Written and illustrated by
Billy Davis

Published by Tangerine Press, an imprint of Scholastic Inc.,
557 Broadway, New York NY 10012

10 9 8 7 6 5 4 3 2 1

ISBN: 0-439-83082-6

So, you like robots? Wanna learn to draw a few? Excellent! You've come to the right place.

In this book you'll be shown, in easy-to-follow steps, 14 different robots, androids, and cyborgs to draw and have a lot of fun with. Who knows, when you're through with these guys maybe you'll be drawing and creating robots on your own!

What are robots, androids, and cyborgs?

What is the difference between a robot and an android anyway? A **robot** is a machine that sometimes looks like a human and can perform different tasks on command. An **android** is a mobile robot not necessarily in human form. **Cyborgs**, however, are entirely different. Cyborgs are human beings whose bodily functions are aided or controlled by robotic technology.

The right tools for the job

To draw robots you'll need a few simple tools: an oscilloscopic two-dimensional image transformer, a zero-movement point calibration meter, hydraulic proprioception guides (in a variety of sizes and weights), safety goggles, and, uh, what's that you say? You don't have an oscilloscopic two-dimensional image transformer? And you don't even know what hydraulic proprioception guides are and what sizes they come in? Oh well, I suppose you can do without them. Try some of these tools. They work just as well.

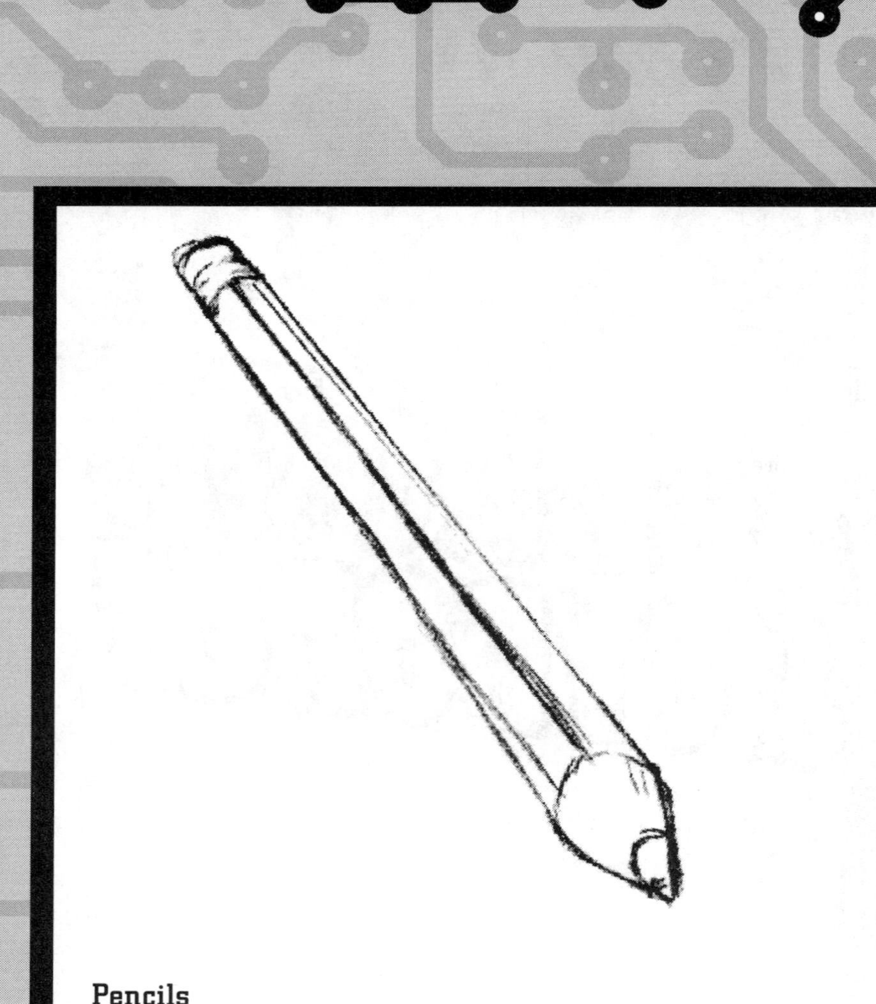

Pencils

Pencils come in different hardnesses from 6B (very very soft with very dark lines) to 2B (not quite as hard and dark) to 2H (very hard point and thin light lines). Have a few pencils of different hardnesses on hand and play around with them to find out which hardness you prefer to draw with. Remember, harder pencils leave lines that might not be easy to erase.

Erasers

An artist's favorite tool is an eraser. The eraser on the end of your pencil will do most of the time, but sometimes you'll need special erasers to help out. A kneaded eraser is soft like dough. It can be molded into shapes to help clean up those hard-to-reach spots in your drawing. A soft crumbly art gum eraser is good to use when you're cleaning up the final drawing. It erases pencil cleanly and safely without tearing paper or smearing the final inking.

Pencil sharpener

Keeping a sharp point on your pencil is very important. You'll have more control over the marks you make and the drawing will be neater and more precise. Have a bunch of sharpened pencils on hand so that you don't have to stop and sharpen as often.

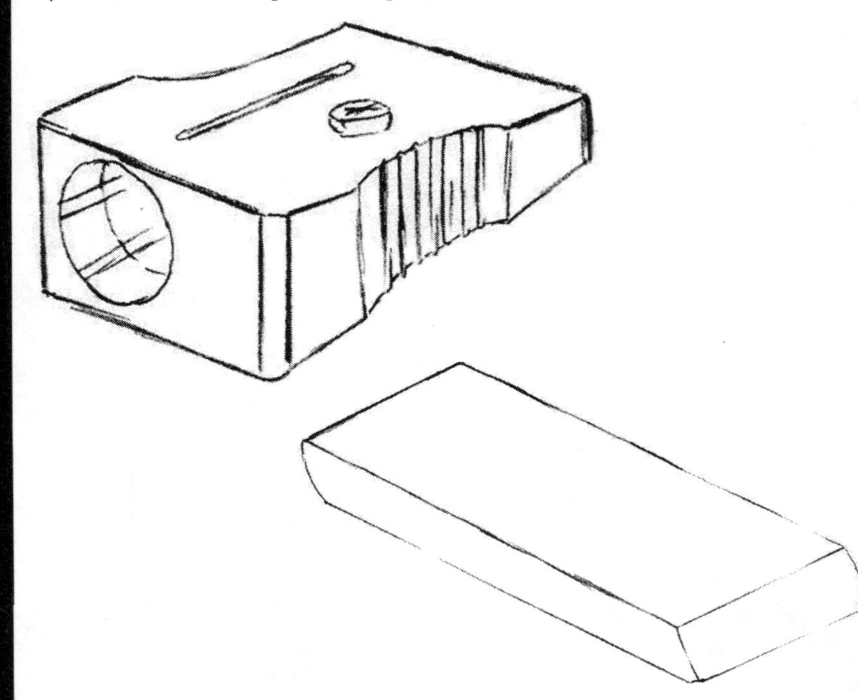

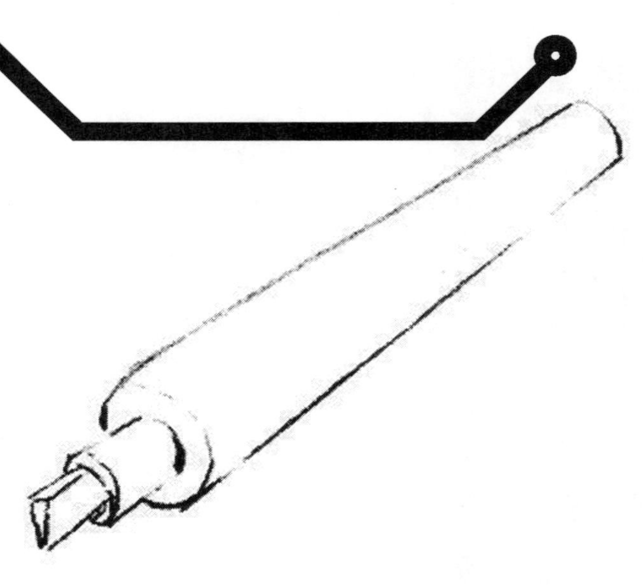

Permanent fine point black marker

After you've gotten the pencil drawing exactly as you want it, you'll need a fine point black marker to carefully go over it and do the finished inking. This is how they do it in the comic book business. When the ink is dry, use an eraser to clean up and remove all the stray pencil marks. You'll need to let the ink dry a few hours to be on the safe side.

Color

Finally, add color to your beautiful drawings. Go wild. Go scary. Use markers or crayons or watercolors. Or maybe even glitter. Or feathers. Okay, so maybe not feathers. You get the idea.

Batteries

The great thing about drawing your own robots is that you don't need batteries.

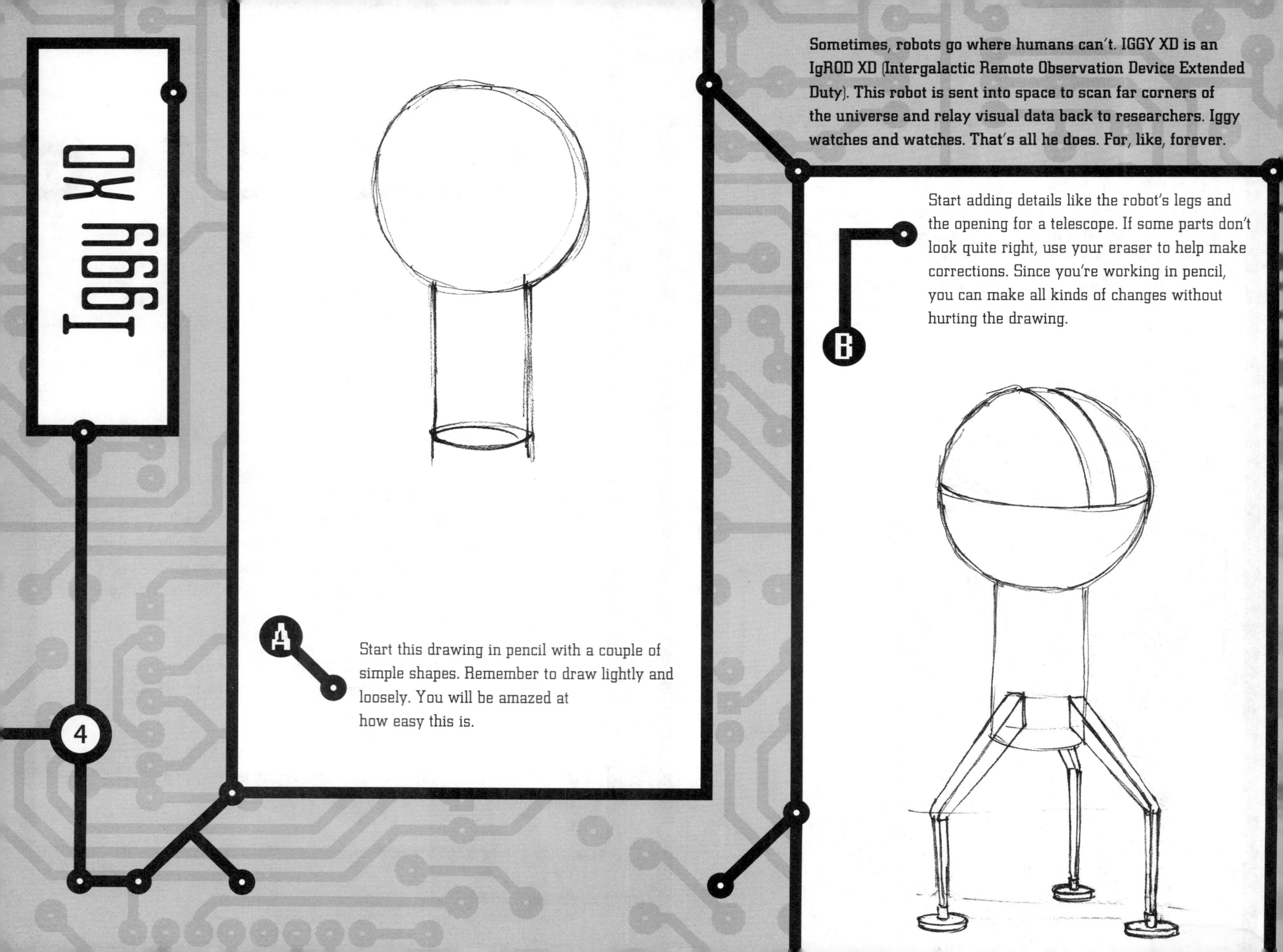

Iggy XD

Sometimes, robots go where humans can't. IGGY XD is an IgROD XD (Intergalactic Remote Observation Device Extended Duty). This robot is sent into space to scan far corners of the universe and relay visual data back to researchers. Iggy watches and watches. That's all he does. For, like, forever.

A

Start this drawing in pencil with a couple of simple shapes. Remember to draw lightly and loosely. You will be amazed at how easy this is.

B

Start adding details like the robot's legs and the opening for a telescope. If some parts don't look quite right, use your eraser to help make corrections. Since you're working in pencil, you can make all kinds of changes without hurting the drawing.

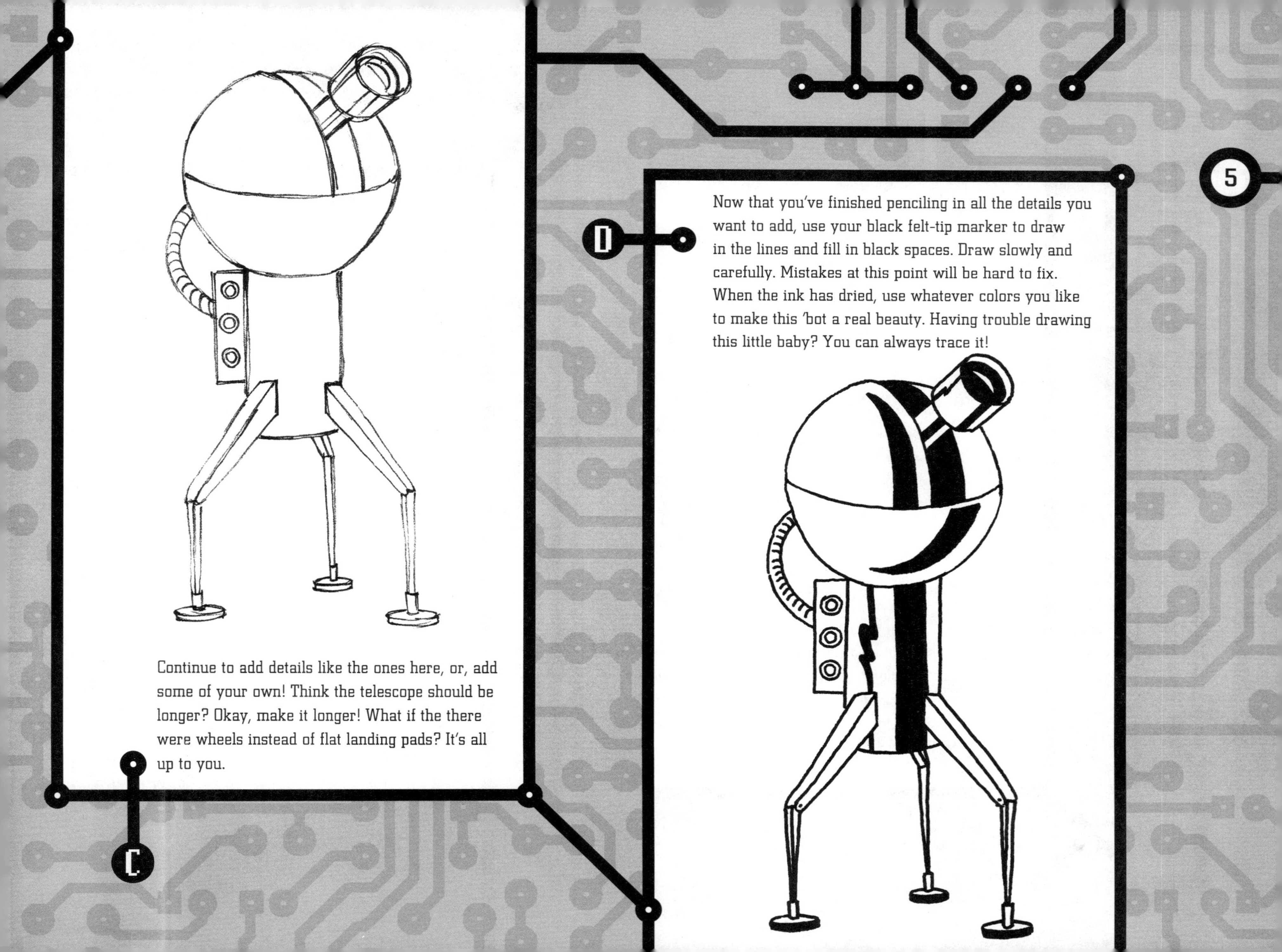

Continue to add details like the ones here, or, add some of your own! Think the telescope should be longer? Okay, make it longer! What if the there were wheels instead of flat landing pads? It's all up to you.

Now that you've finished penciling in all the details you want to add, use your black felt-tip marker to draw in the lines and fill in black spaces. Draw slowly and carefully. Mistakes at this point will be hard to fix. When the ink has dried, use whatever colors you like to make this 'bot a real beauty. Having trouble drawing this little baby? You can always trace it!

Vacumatic

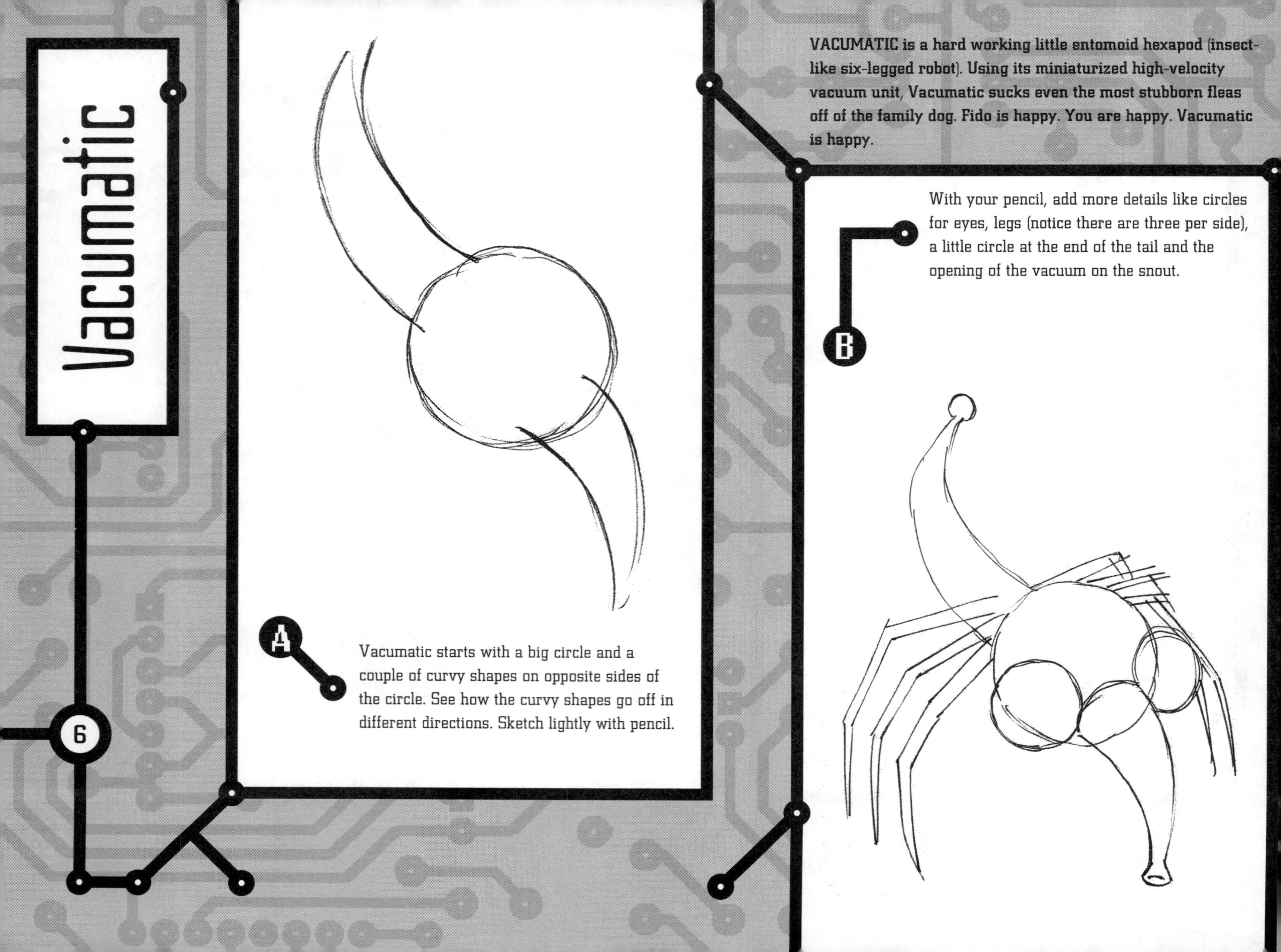

VACUMATIC is a hard working little entomoid hexapod (insect-like six-legged robot). Using its miniaturized high-velocity vacuum unit, Vacumatic sucks even the most stubborn fleas off of the family dog. Fido is happy. You are happy. Vacumatic is happy.

Vacumatic starts with a big circle and a couple of curvy shapes on opposite sides of the circle. See how the curvy shapes go off in different directions. Sketch lightly with pencil.

With your pencil, add more details like circles for eyes, legs (notice there are three per side), a little circle at the end of the tail and the opening of the vacuum on the snout.

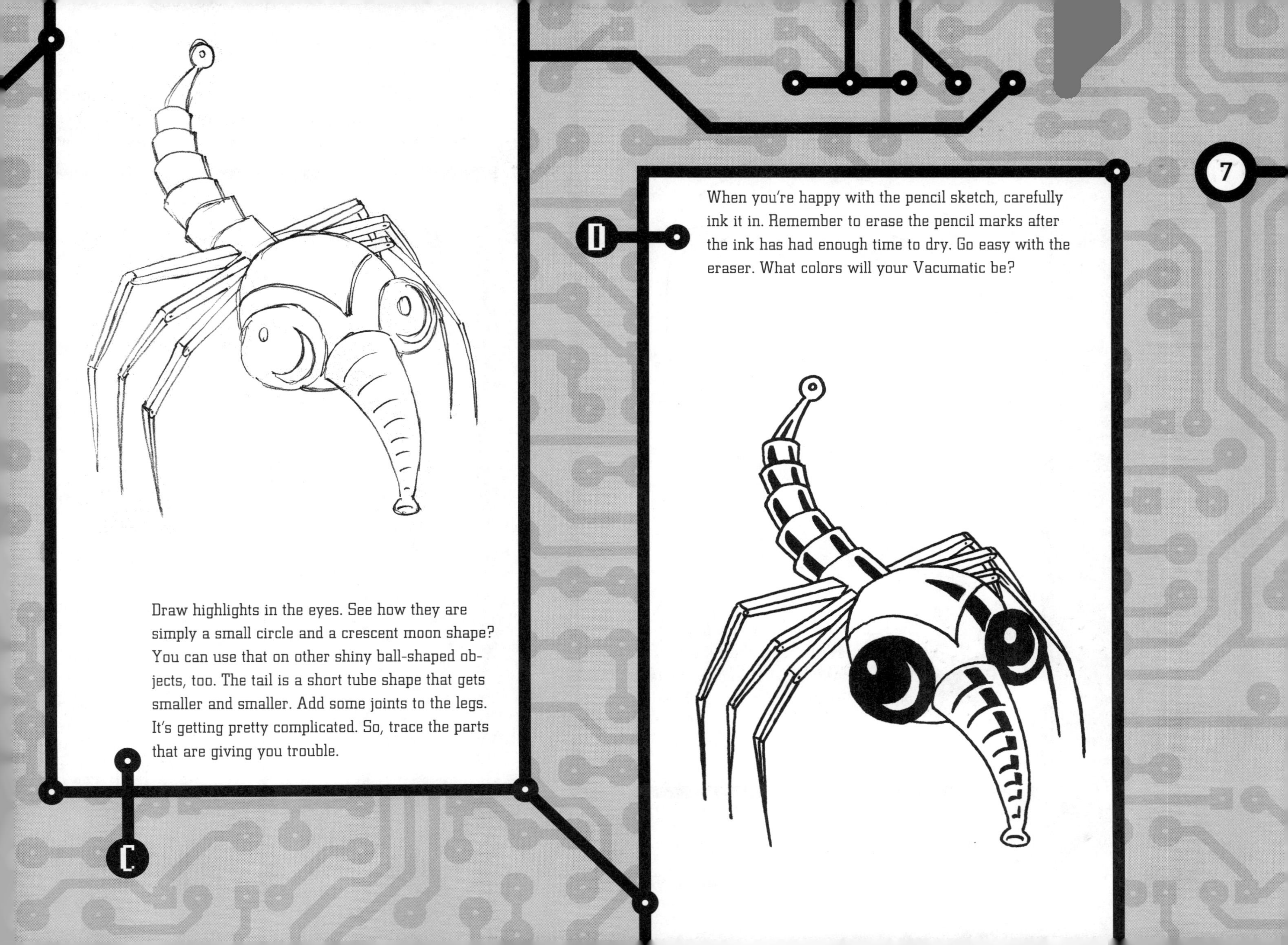

C

Draw highlights in the eyes. See how they are simply a small circle and a crescent moon shape? You can use that on other shiny ball-shaped objects, too. The tail is a short tube shape that gets smaller and smaller. Add some joints to the legs. It's getting pretty complicated. So, trace the parts that are giving you trouble.

D

When you're happy with the pencil sketch, carefully ink it in. Remember to erase the pencil marks after the ink has had enough time to dry. Go easy with the eraser. What colors will your Vacumatic be?

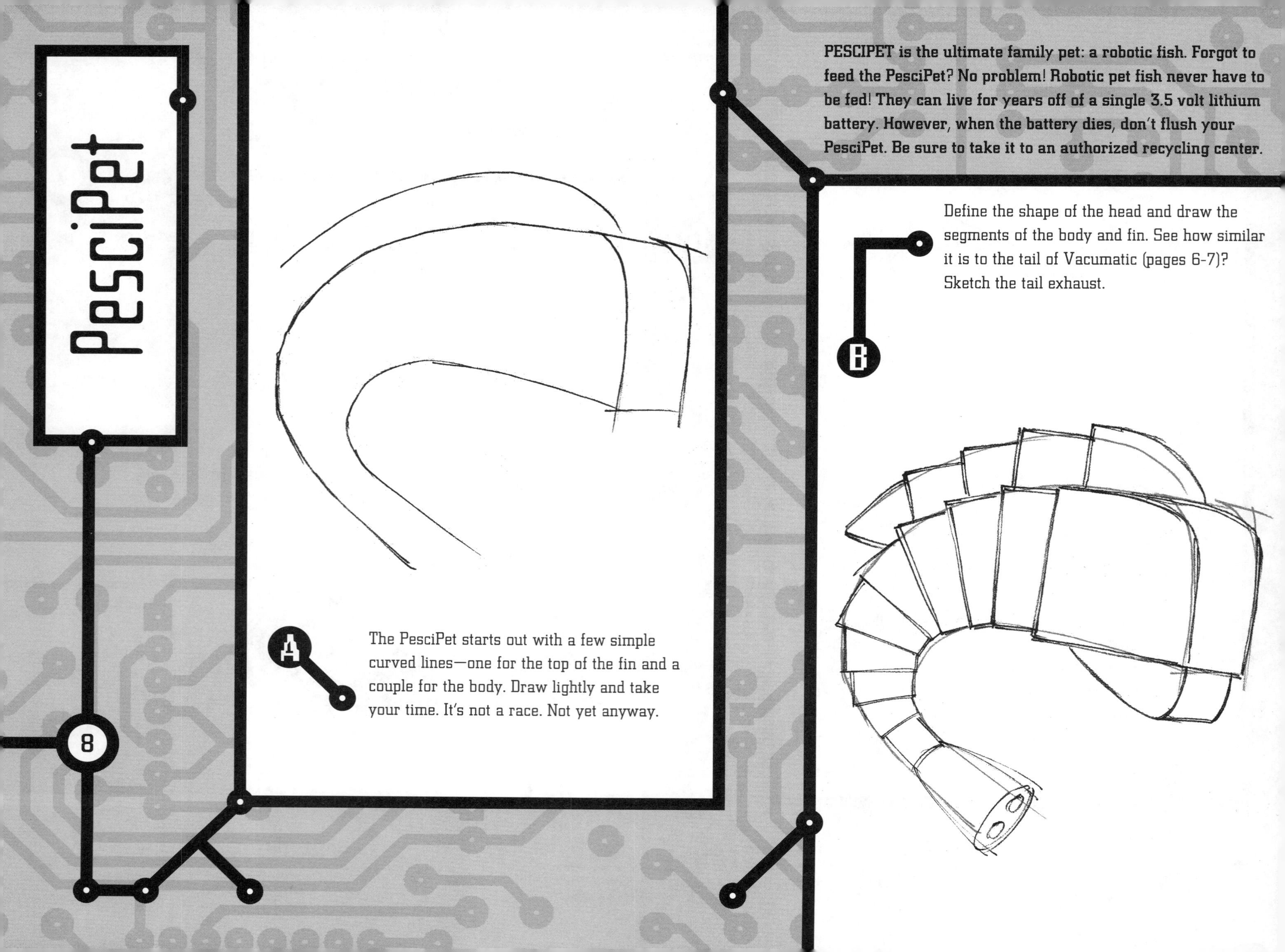

PesciPet

PESCIPET is the ultimate family pet: a robotic fish. Forgot to feed the PesciPet? No problem! Robotic pet fish never have to be fed! They can live for years off of a single 3.5 volt lithium battery. However, when the battery dies, don't flush your PesciPet. Be sure to take it to an authorized recycling center.

A

The PesciPet starts out with a few simple curved lines—one for the top of the fin and a couple for the body. Draw lightly and take your time. It's not a race. Not yet anyway.

B

Define the shape of the head and draw the segments of the body and fin. See how similar it is to the tail of Vacumatic (pages 6-7)? Sketch the tail exhaust.

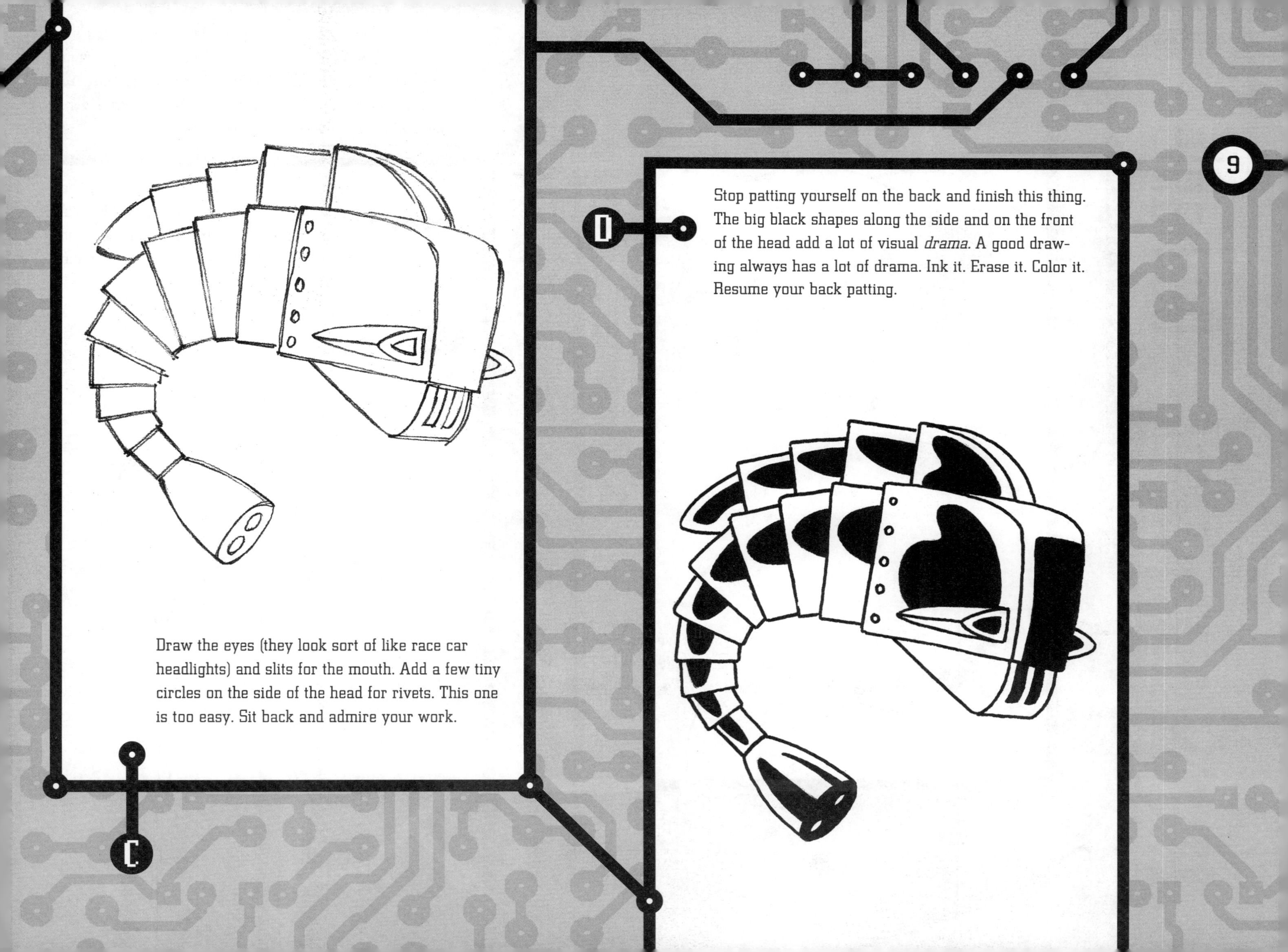

Draw the eyes (they look sort of like race car headlights) and slits for the mouth. Add a few tiny circles on the side of the head for rivets. This one is too easy. Sit back and admire your work.

Stop patting yourself on the back and finish this thing. The big black shapes along the side and on the front of the head add a lot of visual *drama.* A good drawing always has a lot of drama. Ink it. Erase it. Color it. Resume your back patting.

Ocularis

OCULARIS is every school principal's dream—a remote control robotic hall monitor. The patented Peekaboo technology can easily see around corners and in low-light situations. A high-tech laser scanner authenticates hall passes. Nobody gets beyond Ocularis without a proper hall pass.

A

If you stopped at this stage, you'd have a swell mushroom drawing. But you didn't buy *How to Draw Mushrooms, Lichens, and Fungi*, did you? Keep drawing.

B

Begin drawing the two front legs. Put in the joints and feet on the skinny ends. Also sketch a squarish shape on the little body part and add brackets for the eyeball thingies on the underside of the dome.

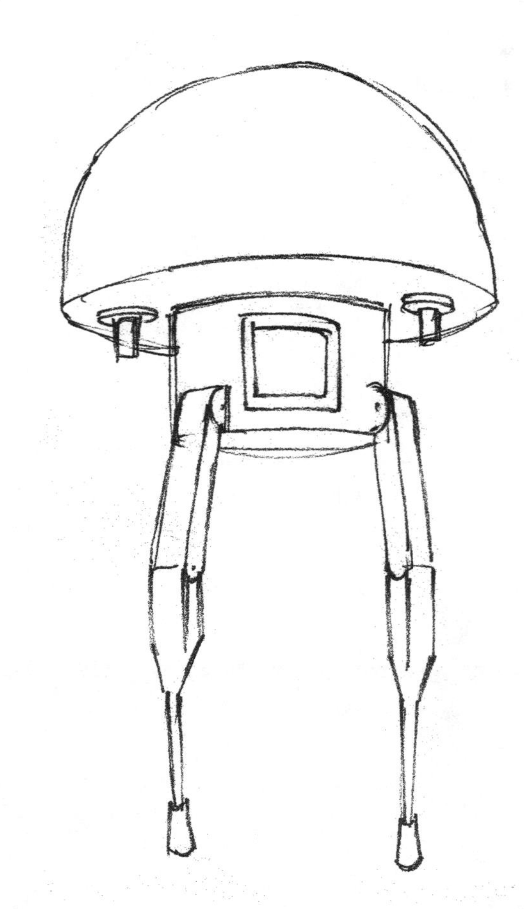

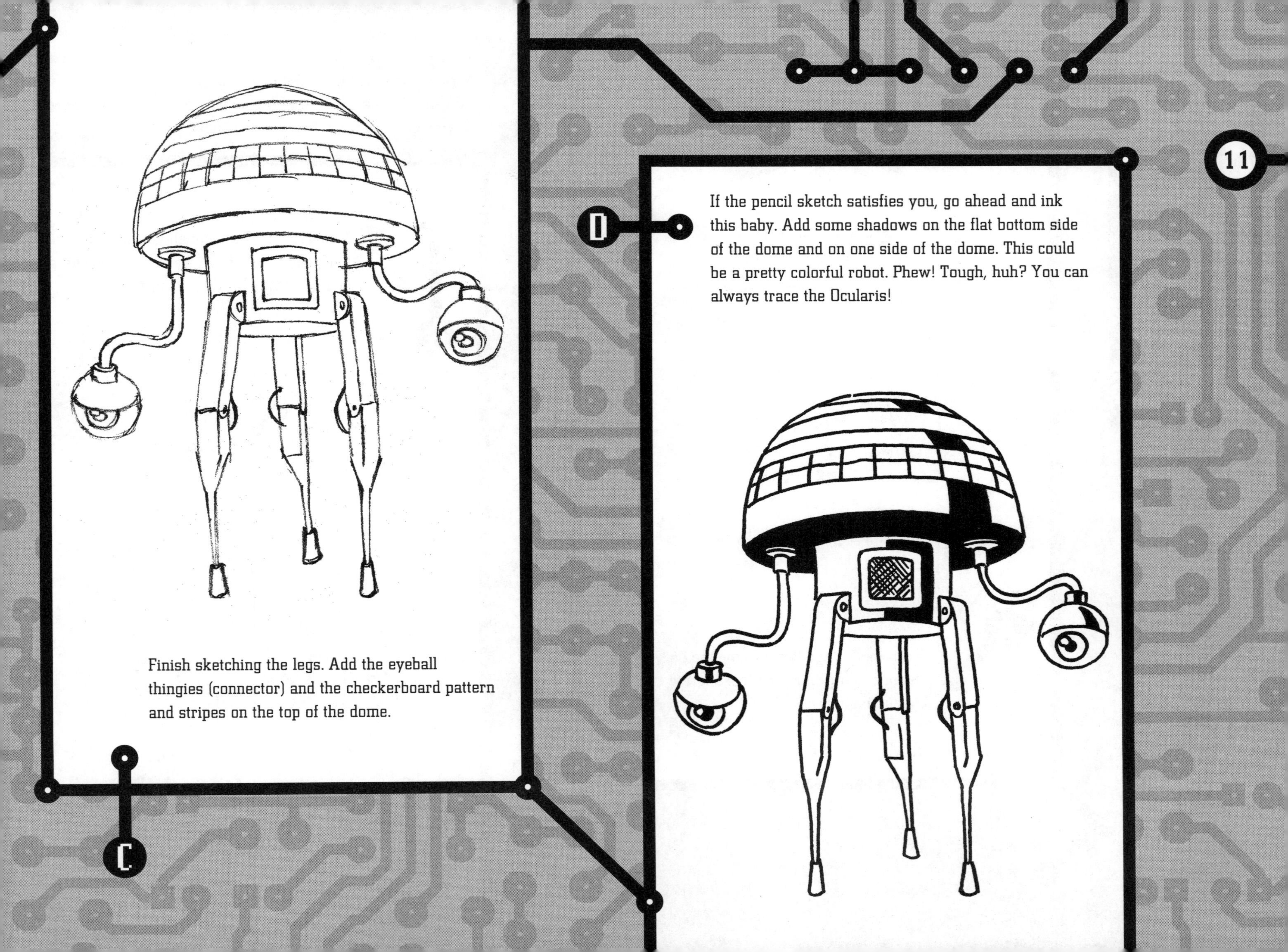

Finish sketching the legs. Add the eyeball thingies (connector) and the checkerboard pattern and stripes on the top of the dome.

If the pencil sketch satisfies you, go ahead and ink this baby. Add some shadows on the flat bottom side of the dome and on one side of the dome. This could be a pretty colorful robot. Phew! Tough, huh? You can always trace the Ocularis!

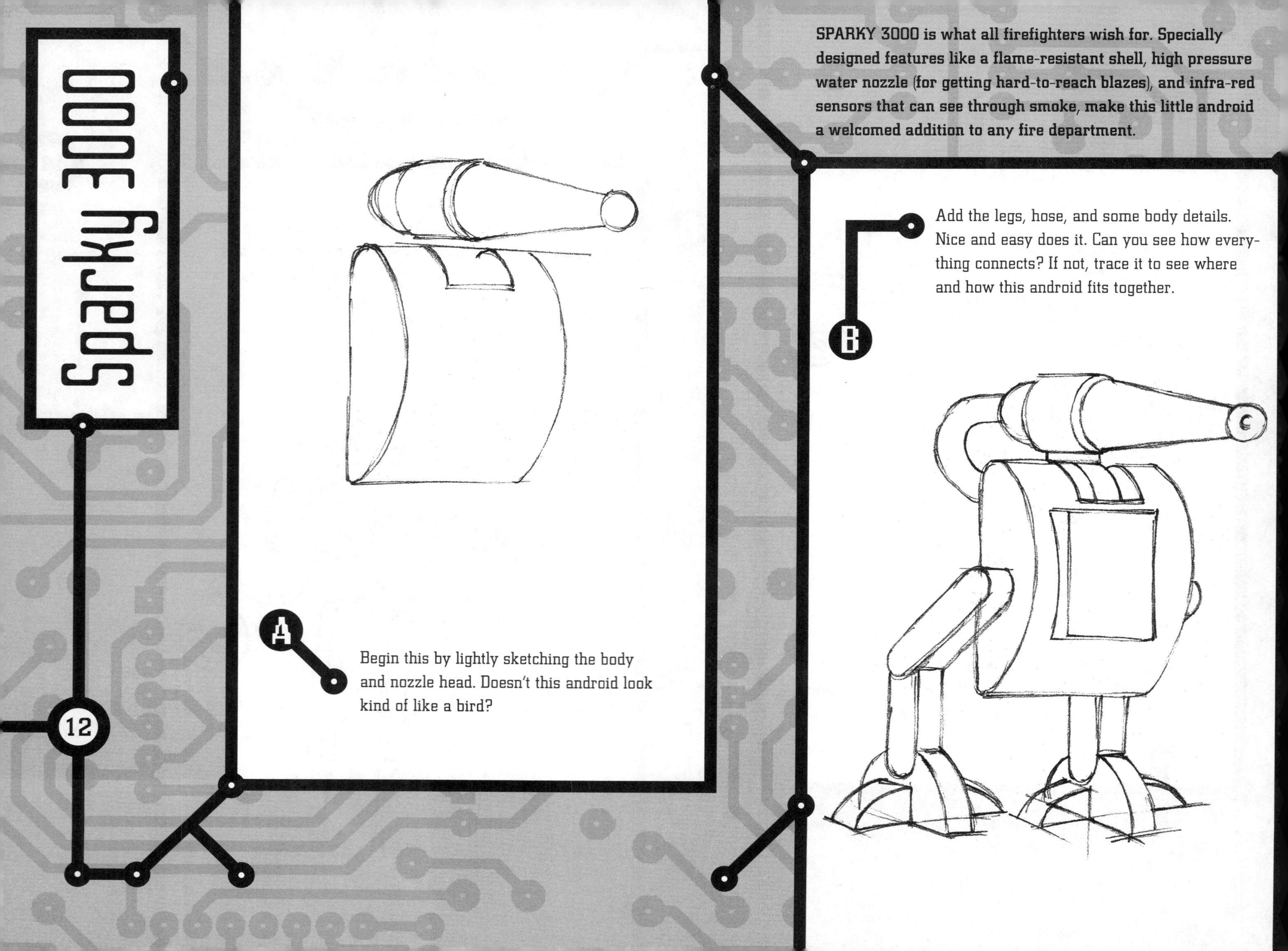

Sparky 3000

SPARKY 3000 is what all firefighters wish for. Specially designed features like a flame-resistant shell, high pressure water nozzle (for getting hard-to-reach blazes), and infra-red sensors that can see through smoke, make this little android a welcomed addition to any fire department.

A

Begin this by lightly sketching the body and nozzle head. Doesn't this android look kind of like a bird?

B

Add the legs, hose, and some body details. Nice and easy does it. Can you see how everything connects? If not, trace it to see where and how this android fits together.

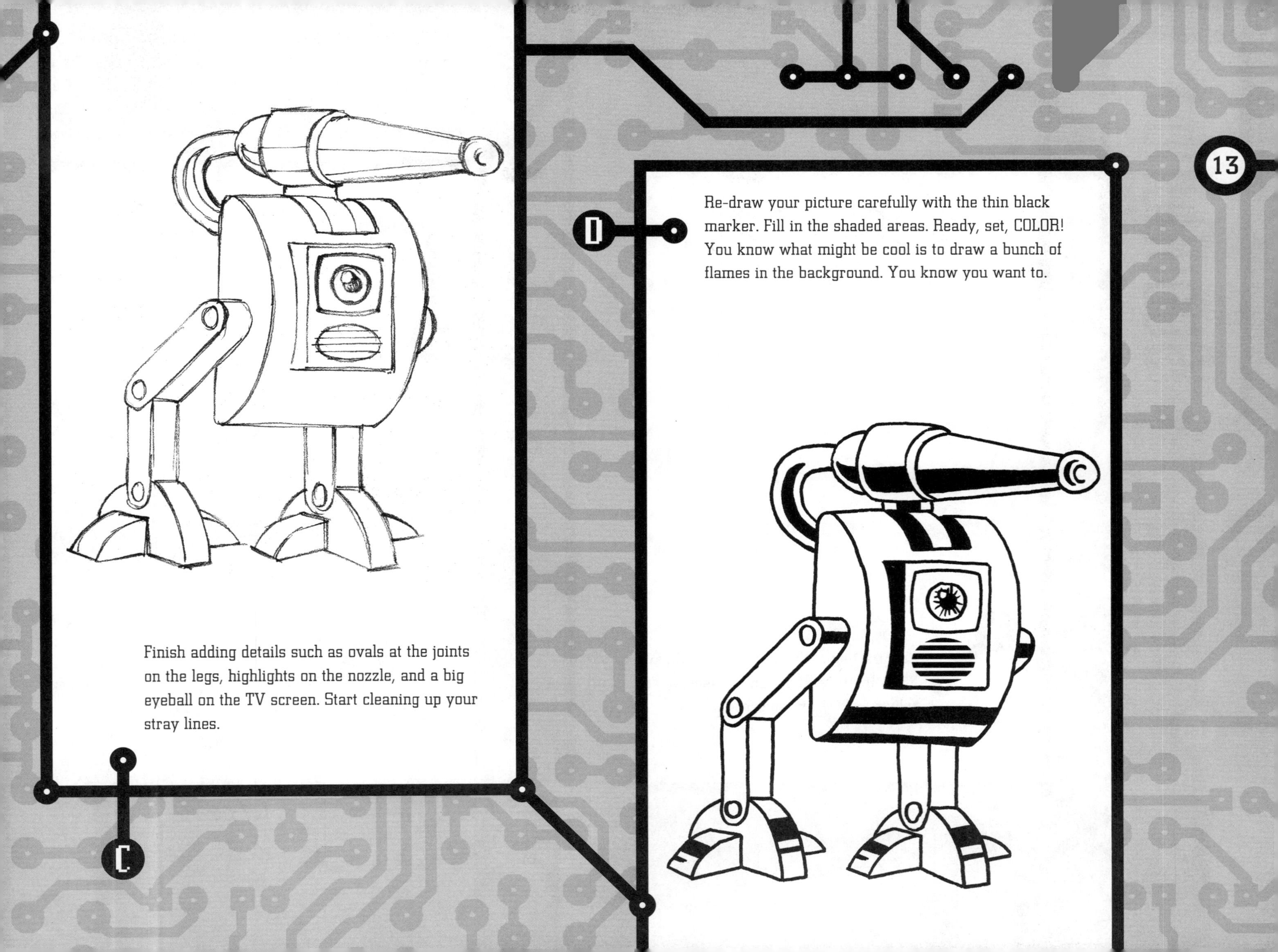

Finish adding details such as ovals at the joints on the legs, highlights on the nozzle, and a big eyeball on the TV screen. Start cleaning up your stray lines.

Re-draw your picture carefully with the thin black marker. Fill in the shaded areas. Ready, set, COLOR! You know what might be cool is to draw a bunch of flames in the background. You know you want to.

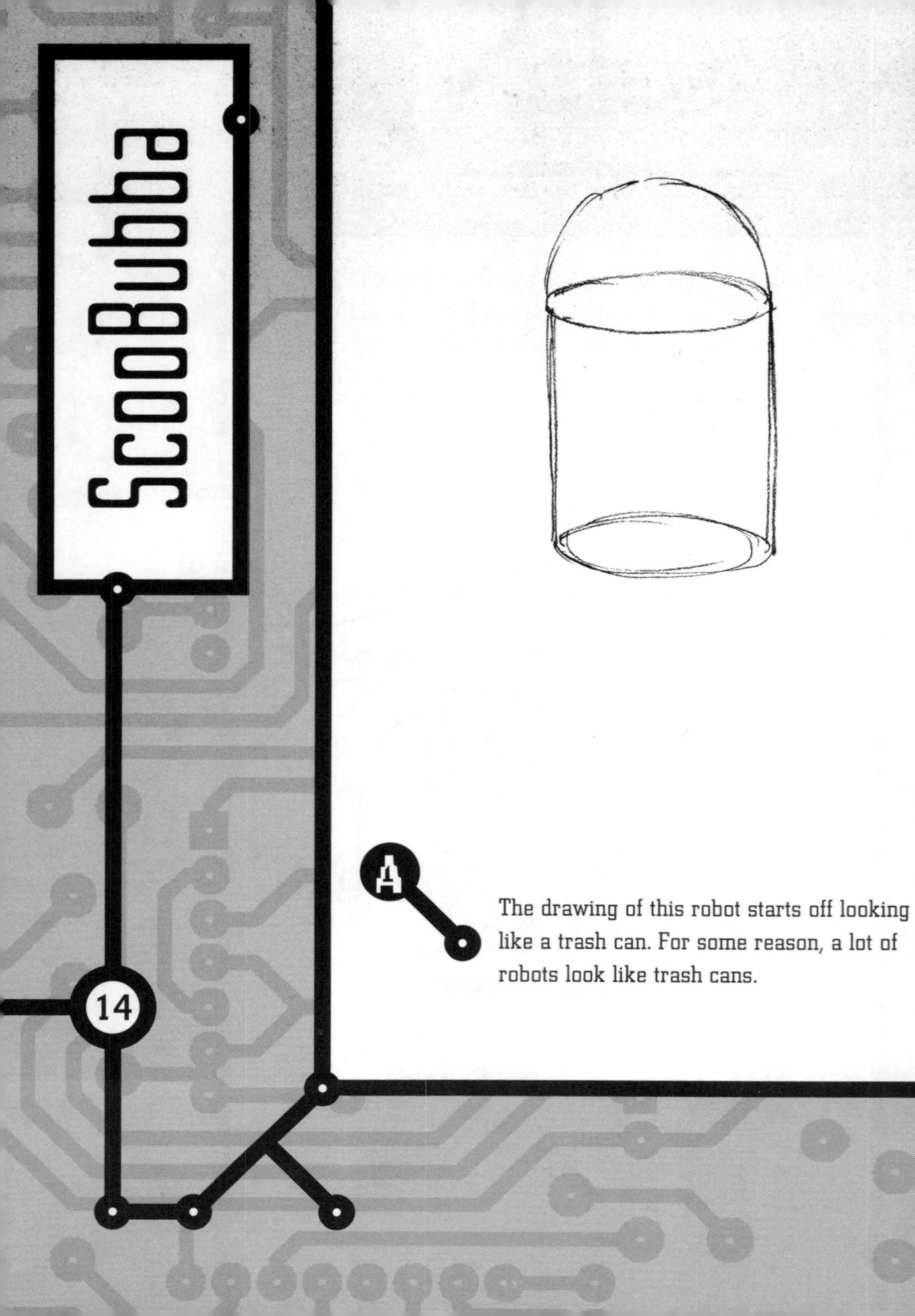

The drawing of this robot starts off looking like a trash can. For some reason, a lot of robots look like trash cans.

SCOOBUBBA is a scuba diver's sub-aquatic personal assistant. Because it is rust resistant and waterproof (up to 300 meters), it is a perfect companion for salt and fresh water diving. Divers can feel safe with ScooBubba's Shark-Away defense circuits (effective on most types of sharks).

Add more details to your trash can, uh, robot. Draw a pointy antenna on the top, a couple of fins on the side, and four octopus-like tentacles on the bottom. Well, in this case, it would be more like a quadrapus.

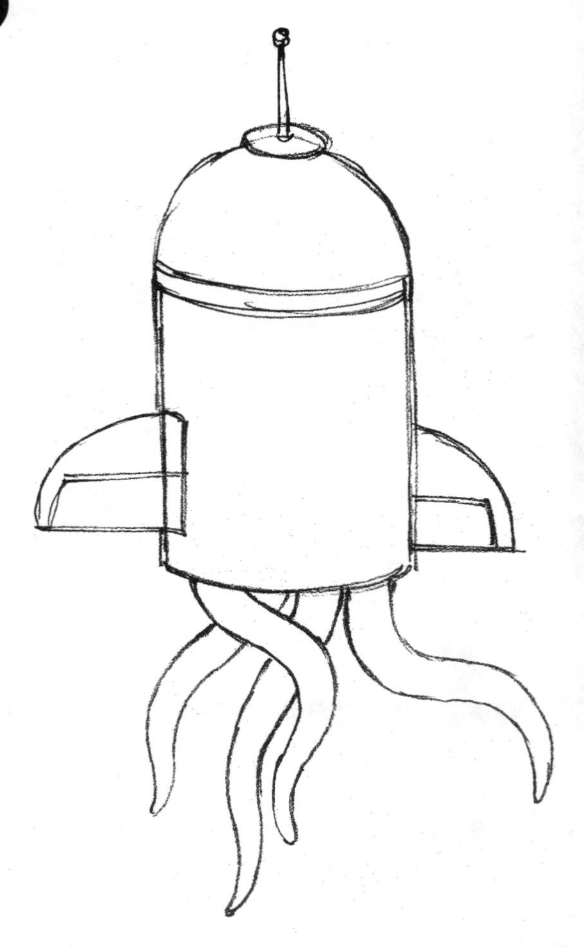

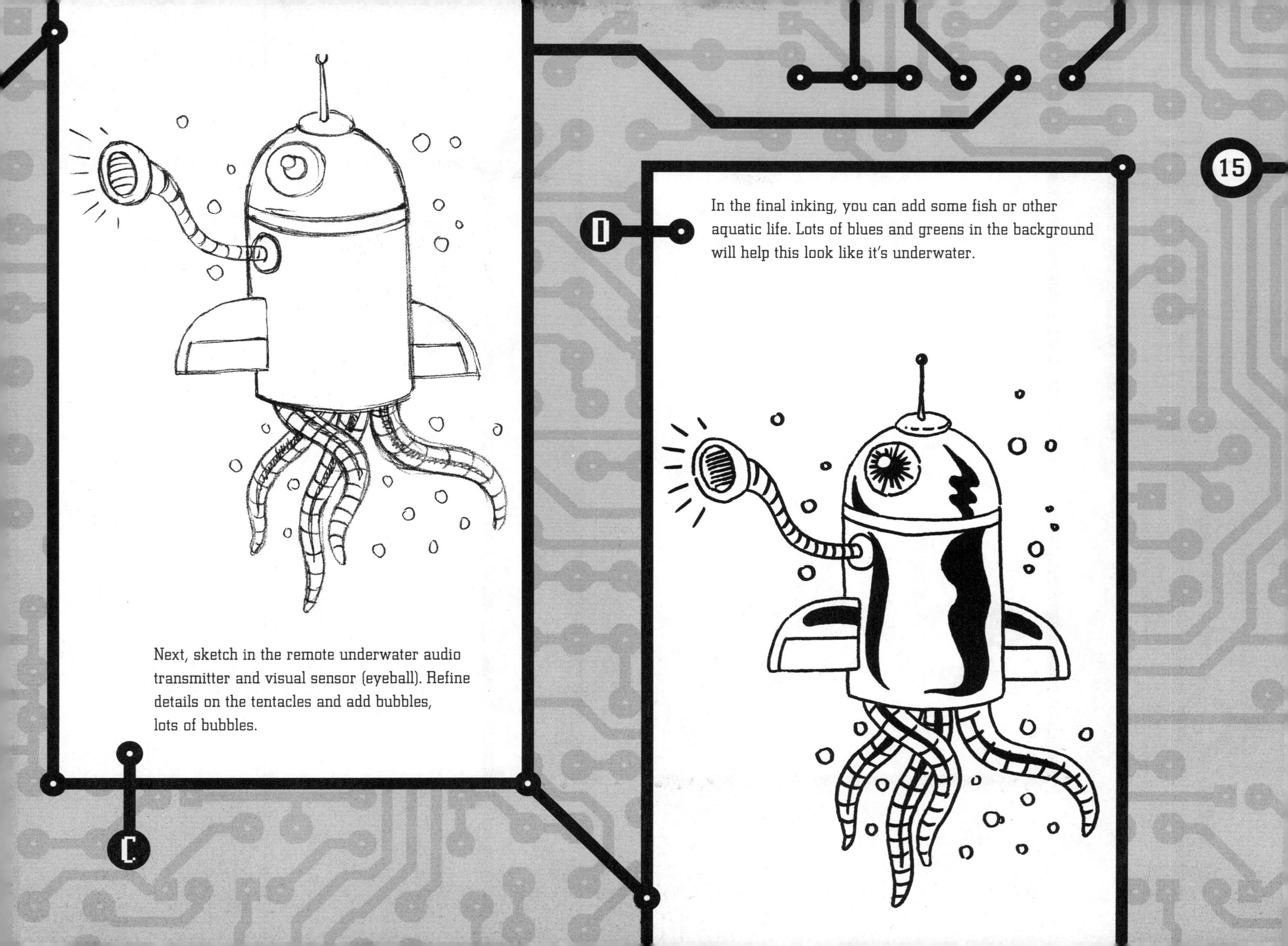
C
Next, sketch in the remote underwater audio transmitter and visual sensor (eyeball). Refine details on the tentacles and add bubbles, lots of bubbles.
D
In the final inking, you can add some fish or other aquatic life. Lots of blues and greens in the background will help this look like it's underwater.

Viktor Cyborg

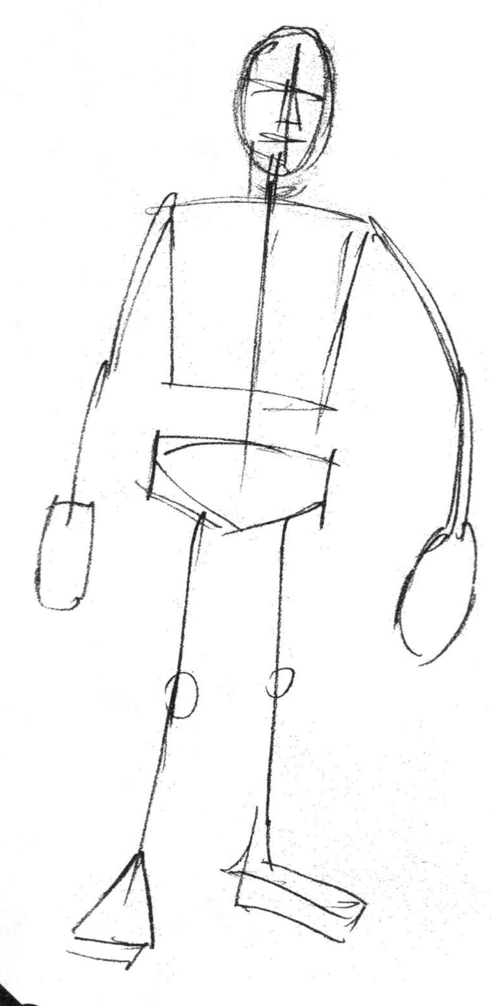

Let's start this cyborg drawing with what is basically a skeleton. Draw loose and take your time.

Every now and then, all of us could use a little help. VIKTOR, the self-powered modular cyborg unit is just the thing. It comes in either left- or right-handed models with an optional night vision ocular device. State laws prohibit using Viktor for an unfair advantage in arm wrestling.

Flesh out the body and some of the shapes that define what the cyborg parts look like.

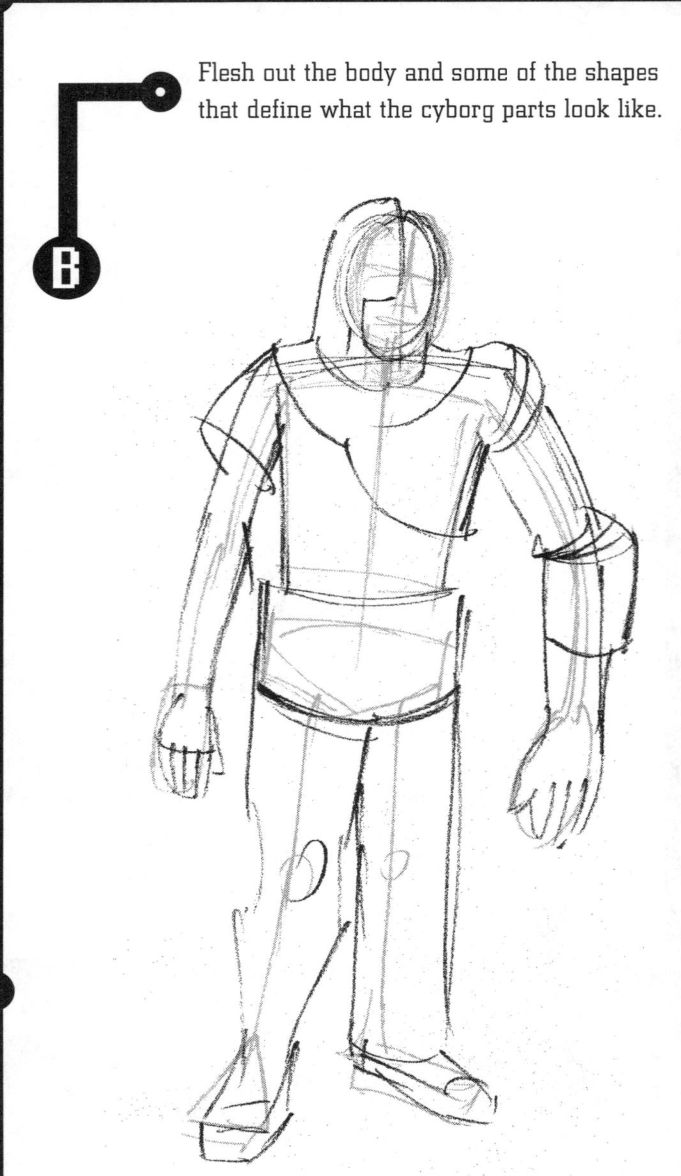

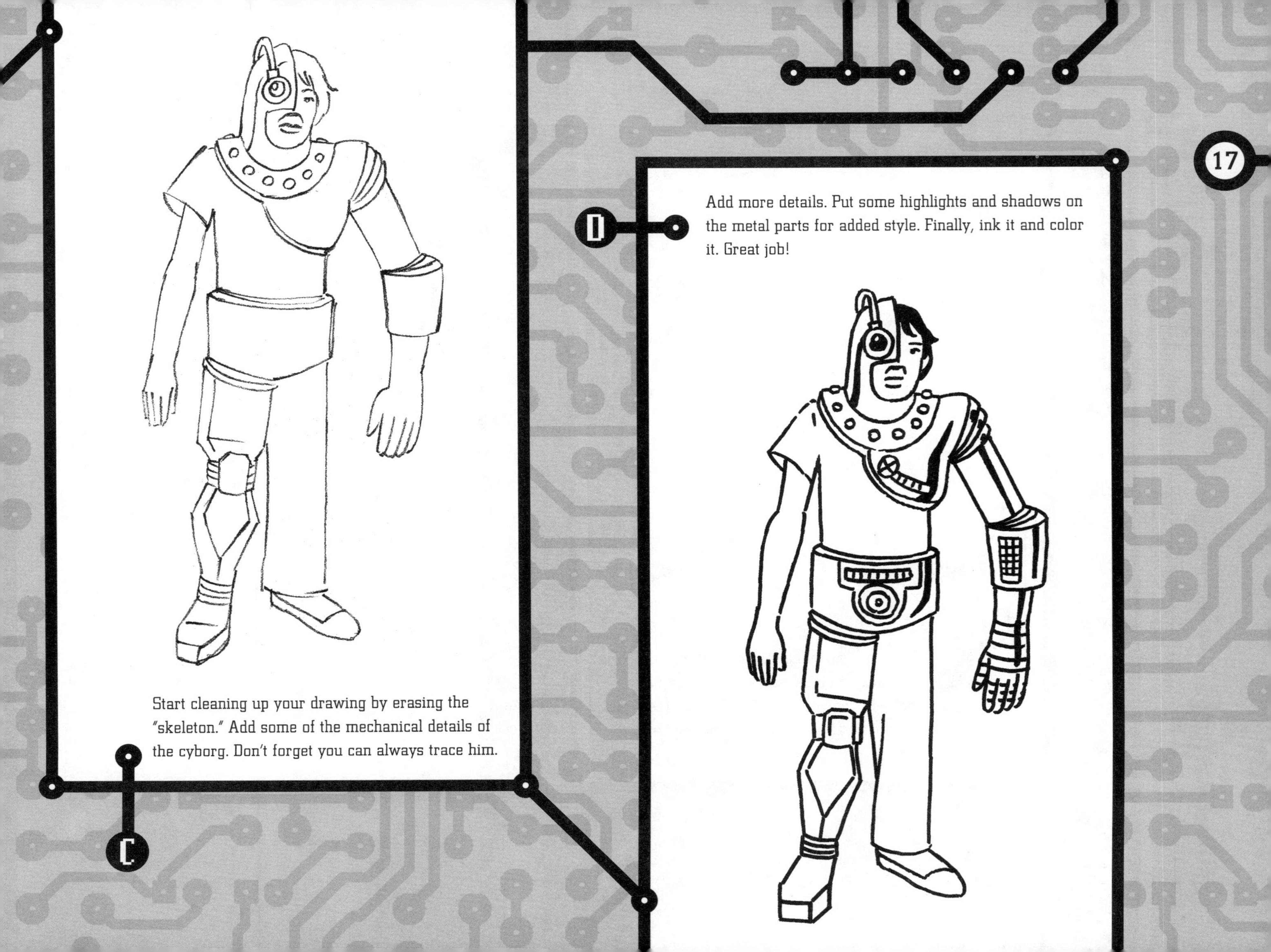

C

Start cleaning up your drawing by erasing the "skeleton." Add some of the mechanical details of the cyborg. Don't forget you can always trace him.

D

Add more details. Put some highlights and shadows on the metal parts for added style. Finally, ink it and color it. Great job!

Bi-Ped Ed

BI-PED ED's enhanced safety programming makes this the best robotic crossing guard in the country. Okay, it's the only robotic crossing guard in the country. It can monitor traffic flow and volume while safely ushering you across the busiest of streets.

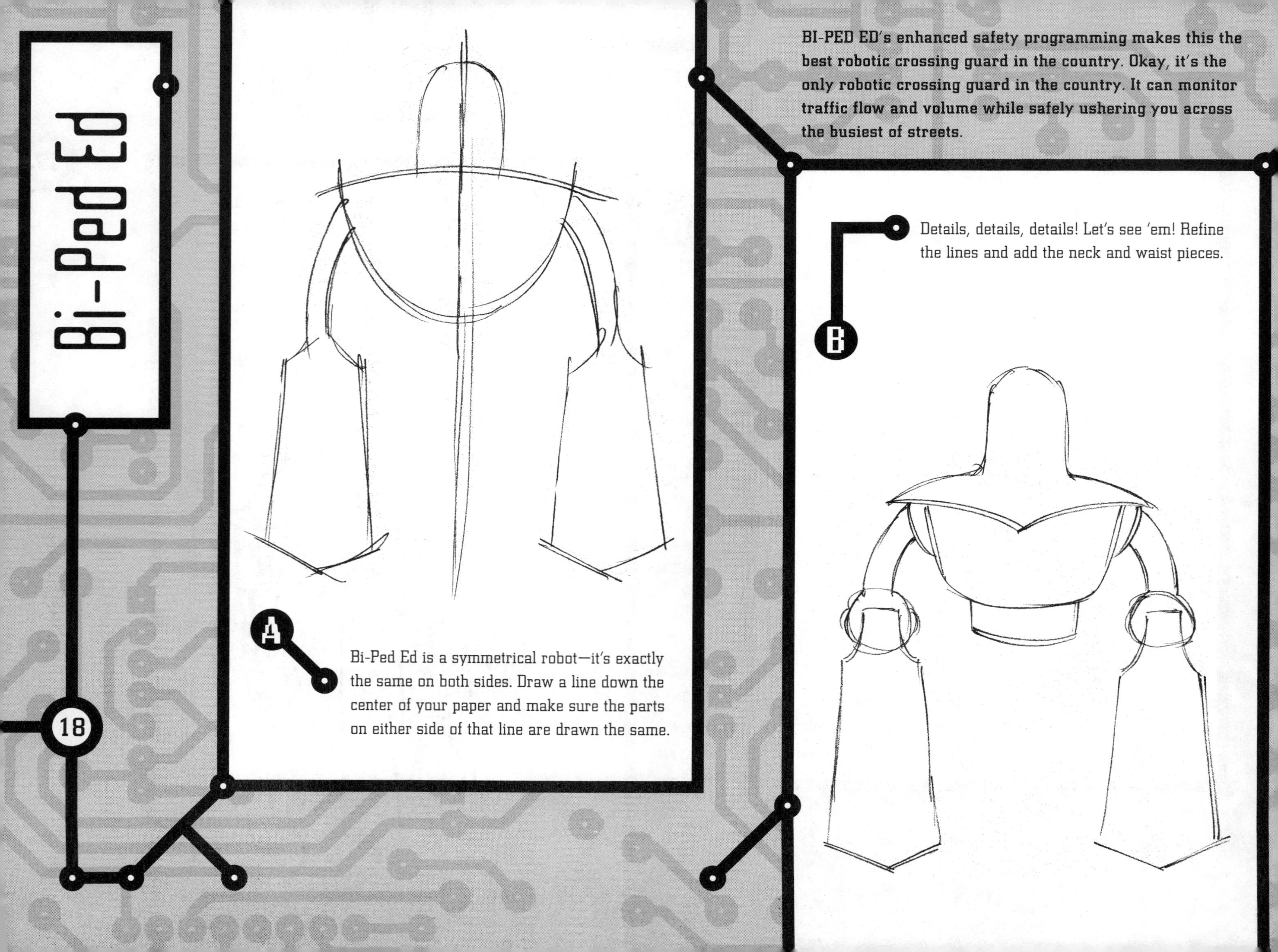

Bi-Ped Ed is a symmetrical robot—it's exactly the same on both sides. Draw a line down the center of your paper and make sure the parts on either side of that line are drawn the same.

Details, details, details! Let's see 'em! Refine the lines and add the neck and waist pieces.

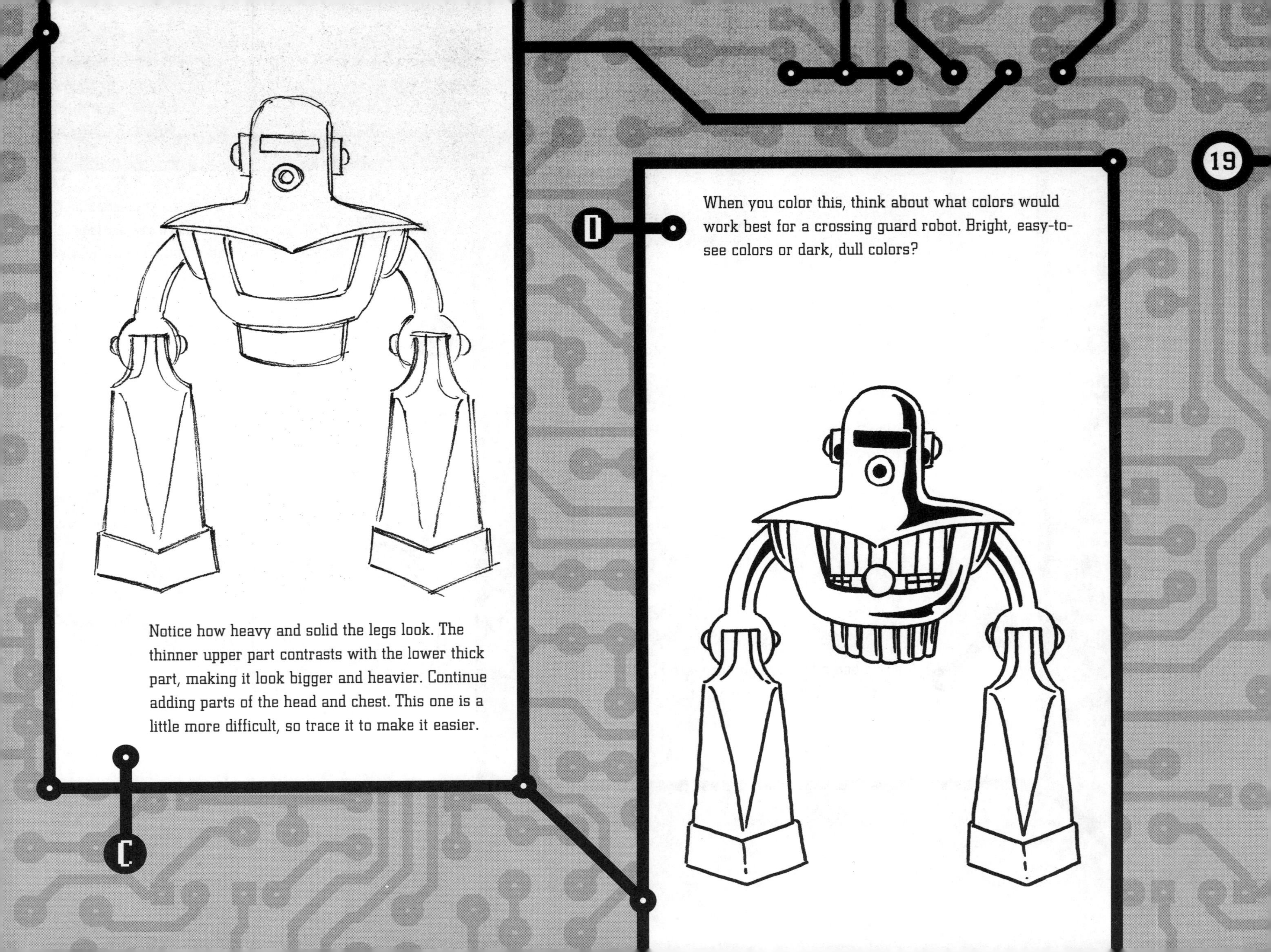

Notice how heavy and solid the legs look. The thinner upper part contrasts with the lower thick part, making it look bigger and heavier. Continue adding parts of the head and chest. This one is a little more difficult, so trace it to make it easier.

C

D

When you color this, think about what colors would work best for a crossing guard robot. Bright, easy-to-see colors or dark, dull colors?

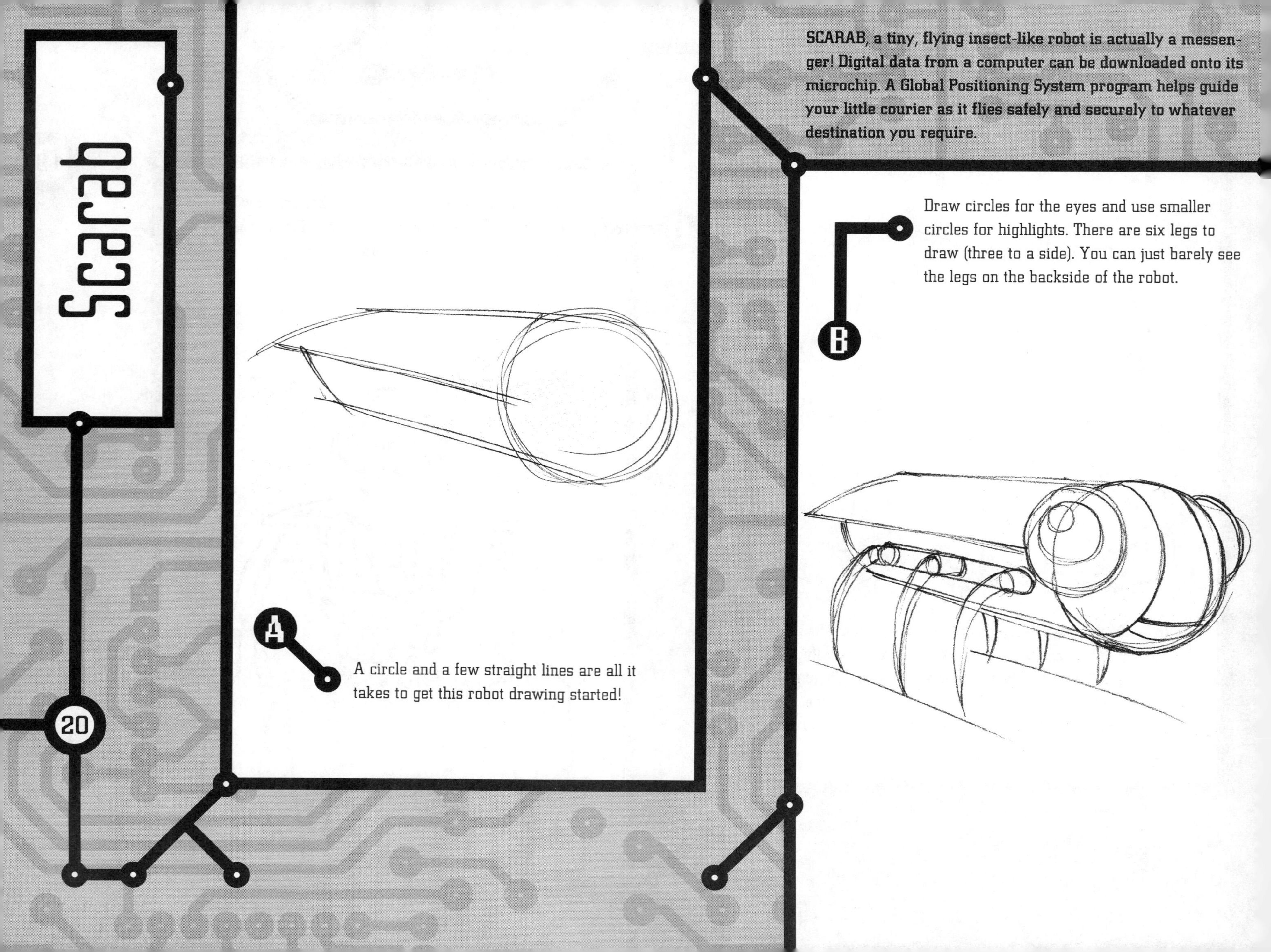

Scarab

SCARAB, a tiny, flying insect-like robot is actually a messenger! Digital data from a computer can be downloaded onto its microchip. A Global Positioning System program helps guide your little courier as it flies safely and securely to whatever destination you require.

A

A circle and a few straight lines are all it takes to get this robot drawing started!

B

Draw circles for the eyes and use smaller circles for highlights. There are six legs to draw (three to a side). You can just barely see the legs on the backside of the robot.

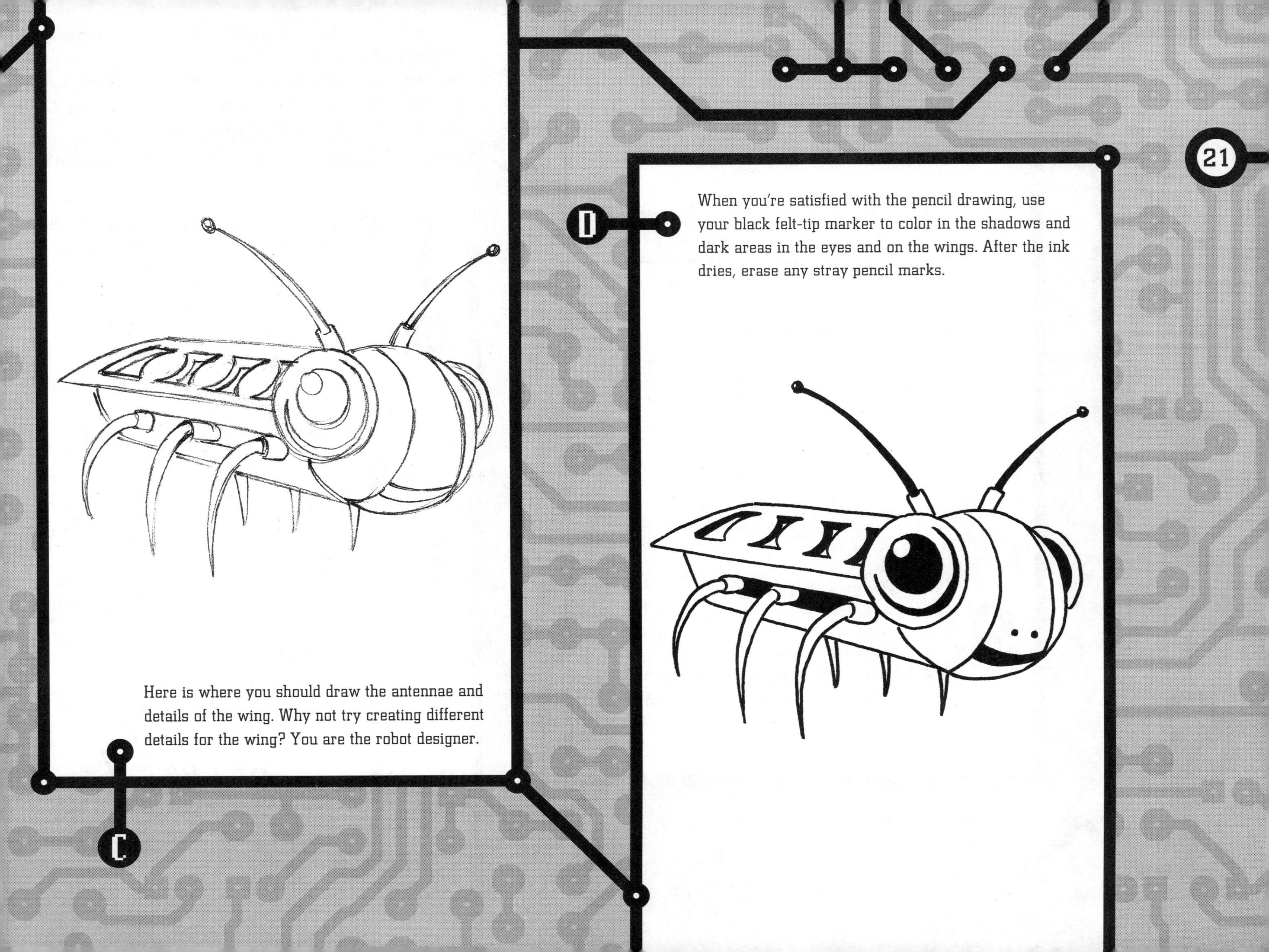

C

Here is where you should draw the antennae and details of the wing. Why not try creating different details for the wing? You are the robot designer.

D

When you're satisfied with the pencil drawing, use your black felt-tip marker to color in the shadows and dark areas in the eyes and on the wings. After the ink dries, erase any stray pencil marks.

DeeJay GJ

You're gonna bust a move when this bling dog invades your crib. DEEJAY GJ is the world's only street-certified turntablist/Rap/Hip Hop robot. Its twin direct drive, quartz-locked turntables have micro-balancing adjustors for reliable pitch, and it also features feather-touch stop/start. Word.

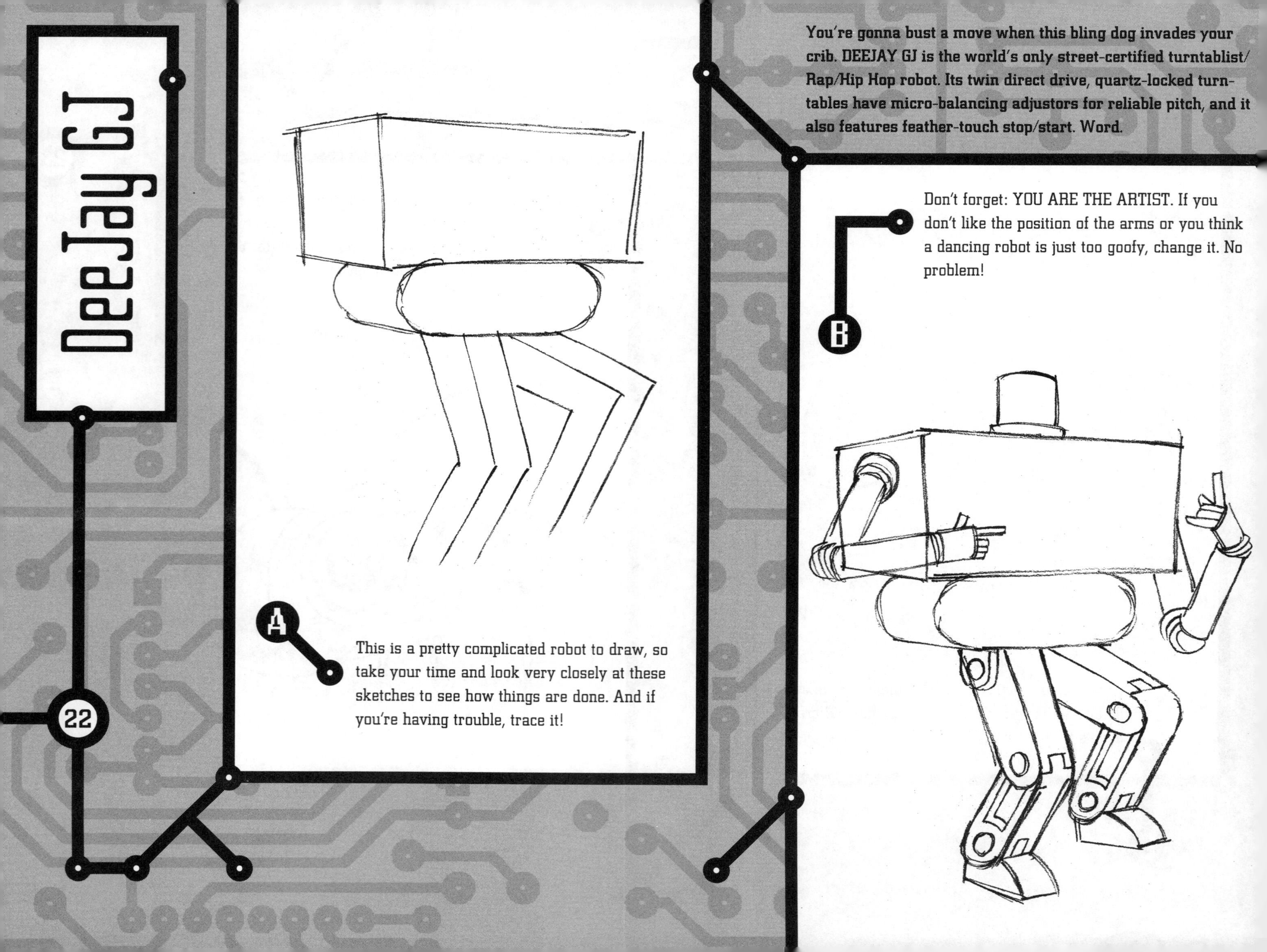

This is a pretty complicated robot to draw, so take your time and look very closely at these sketches to see how things are done. And if you're having trouble, trace it!

Don't forget: YOU ARE THE ARTIST. If you don't like the position of the arms or you think a dancing robot is just too goofy, change it. No problem!

Sketch out the turntables and controls. This is pretty tricky. Notice the turntables are not perfect circles but are more oval in shape.

C

D

Carefully re-ink the drawing and fill in the black areas of the records and other shadows. When you color this in, give it plenty of gizmos and gadgets!

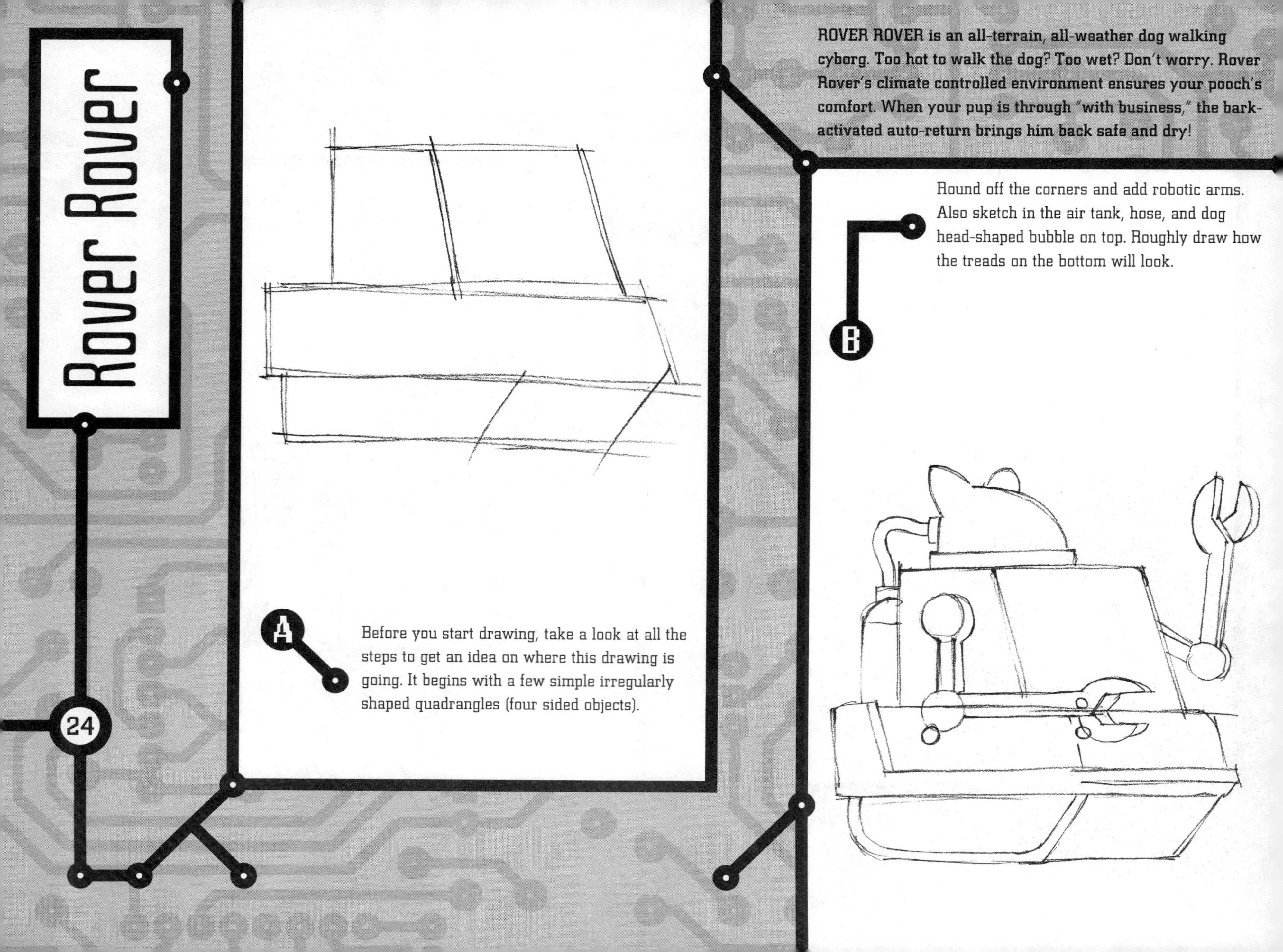

Rover Rover

ROVER ROVER is an all-terrain, all-weather dog walking cyborg. Too hot to walk the dog? Too wet? Don't worry. Rover Rover's climate controlled environment ensures your pooch's comfort. When your pup is through "with business," the bark-activated auto-return brings him back safe and dry!

A

Before you start drawing, take a look at all the steps to get an idea on where this drawing is going. It begins with a few simple irregularly shaped quadrangles (four sided objects).

B

Round off the corners and add robotic arms. Also sketch in the air tank, hose, and dog head-shaped bubble on top. Roughly draw how the treads on the bottom will look.

C

Add the tread details with wheels (simple oval shapes). Finish drawing the arms by adding pistons and screw heads. If you're confused on all these parts, break out the tracing paper and trace this little robot dude.

D

Draw the dog head in the bubble (this is a German Shepherd, but any canine will do). Add the radar screen on the front panel. Now ink it in and color it whatever color you want.

HOMEROID's powerful servomotors make this Domestic Assistant Android a must-have for any home. Homeroid's special skills include: pickle jar opening, aluminum can crushing, and garbage bag removal. If Homeroid had a mouth, you'd see him smiling through each and every task.

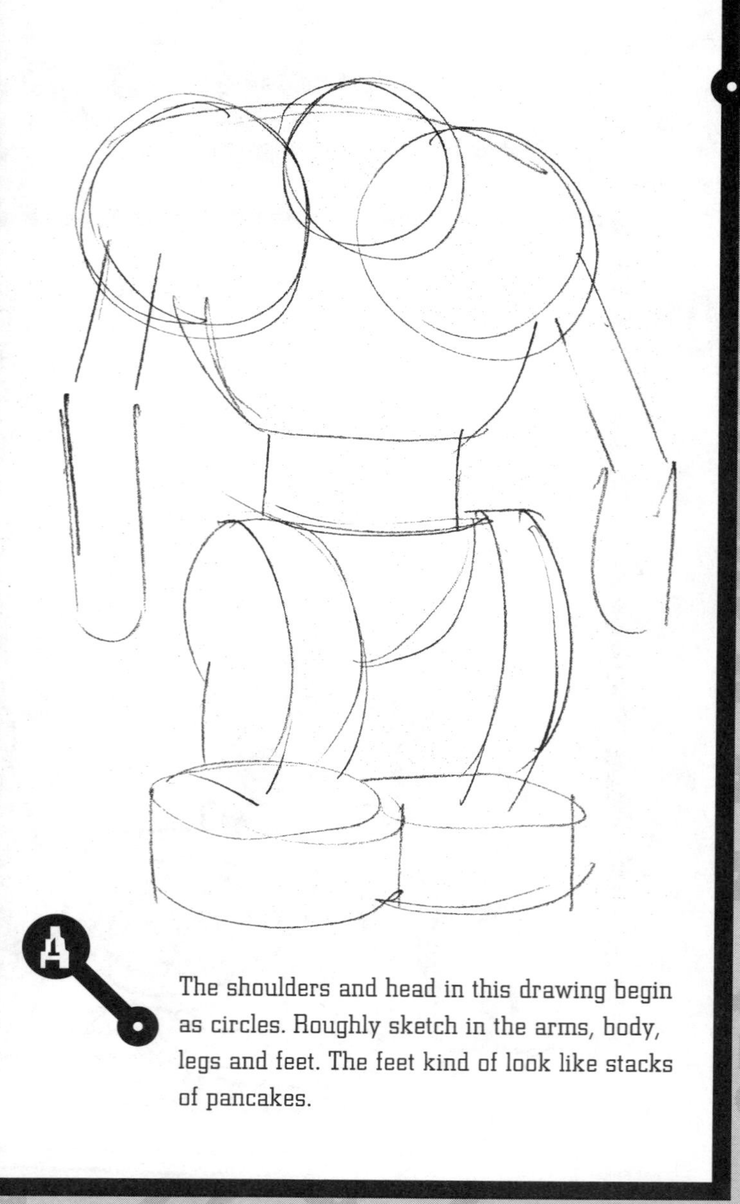

A

The shoulders and head in this drawing begin as circles. Roughly sketch in the arms, body, legs and feet. The feet kind of look like stacks of pancakes.

B

Add definition to to the upper body. Draw the elbow joints and fingers. Draw the design on the chest plate.

In this step, draw the face and other details throughout the rest of the robot's body. Wow, this one's tough with all the little pieces and parts. If you're having trouble, break out the tracing paper!

C

D

Finally, draw the control panel on the chest and add highlights and shadows. Since this is a household robot, you'll probably want to color it to match the curtains or the carpet.

Agribot v2

Farmers are now using AGRIBOT V2—a flying harvester android. Agribot flies low over the fields cutting down produce with lasers and lifting it with mechanical legs into its cargo area. The robot then flies directly to market delivering fresher, healthier food, like spinach. Oh, boy!

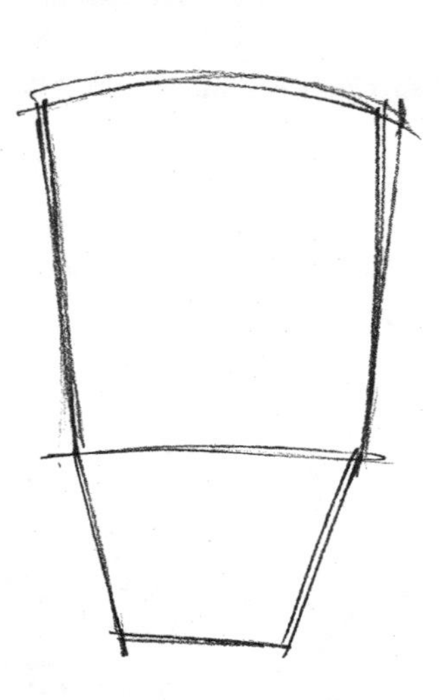

A

An easy first step. Draw two quadrangles. The top one is larger and has a slight curve on the top edge. The one on the bottom is smaller and its bottom side is shorter.

B

Draw a few details on the body of the robot. Add eyes (or headlights), wings, and curvy lines on the front part. See how the curved lines have just about the same curve as the top edge of the front part? It's important for your Agribot to look rounded.

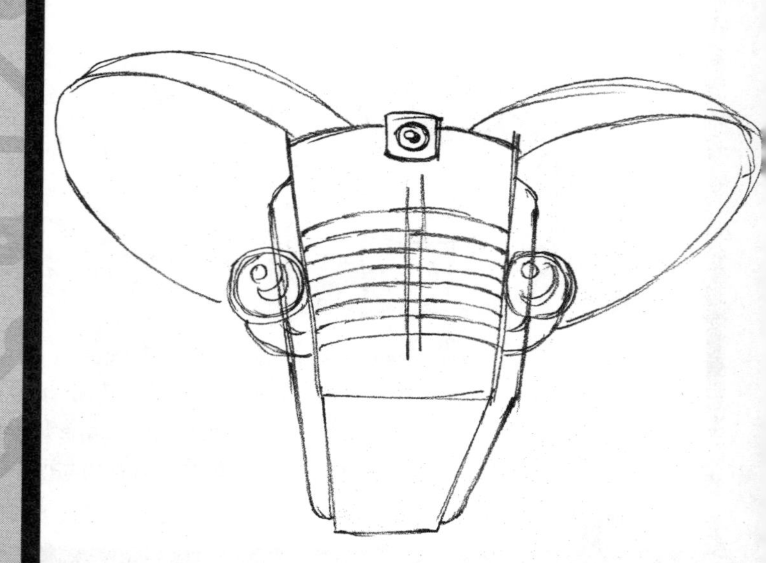

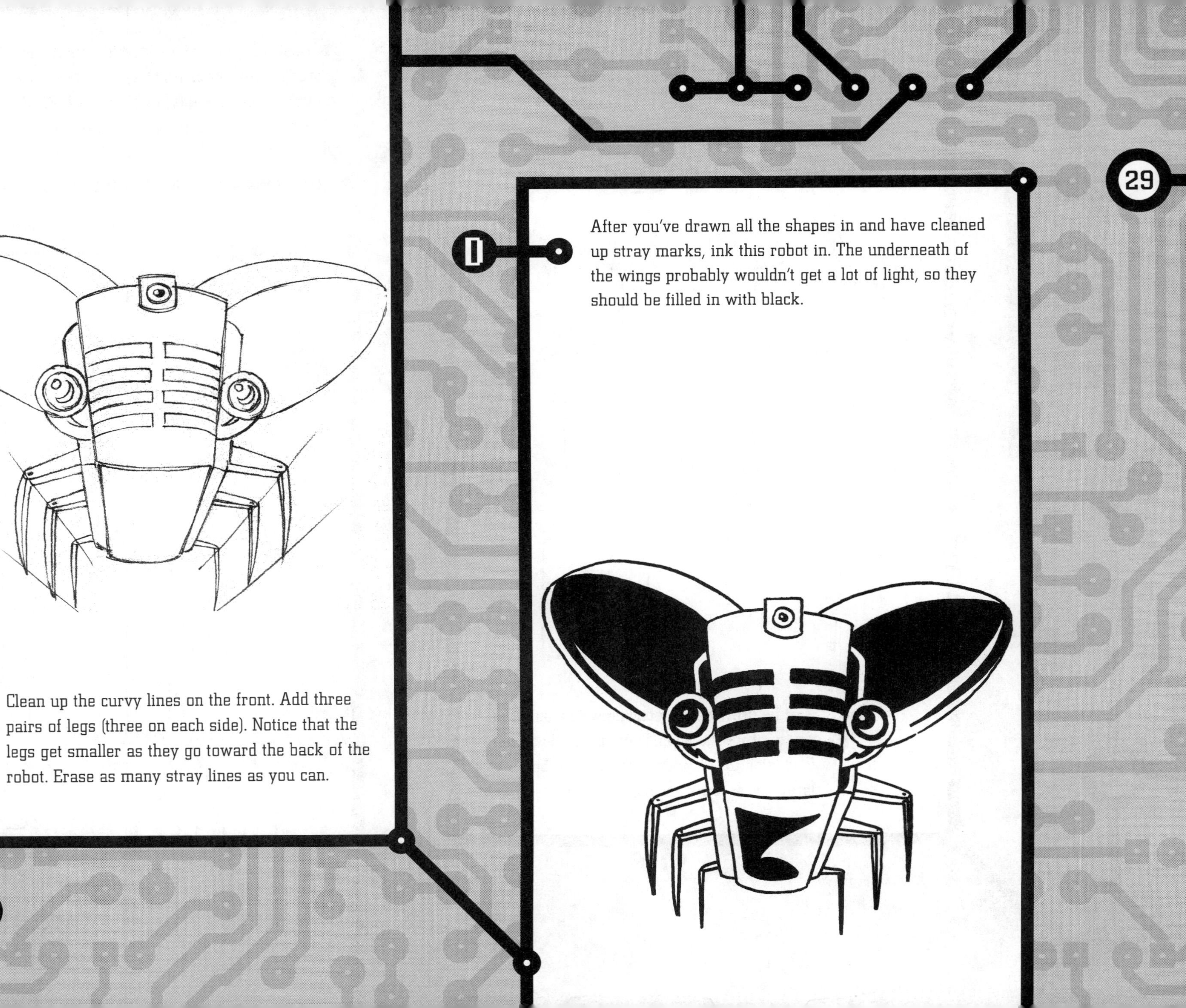

Clean up the curvy lines on the front. Add three pairs of legs (three on each side). Notice that the legs get smaller as they go toward the back of the robot. Erase as many stray lines as you can.

After you've drawn all the shapes in and have cleaned up stray marks, ink this robot in. The underneath of the wings probably wouldn't get a lot of light, so they should be filled in with black.

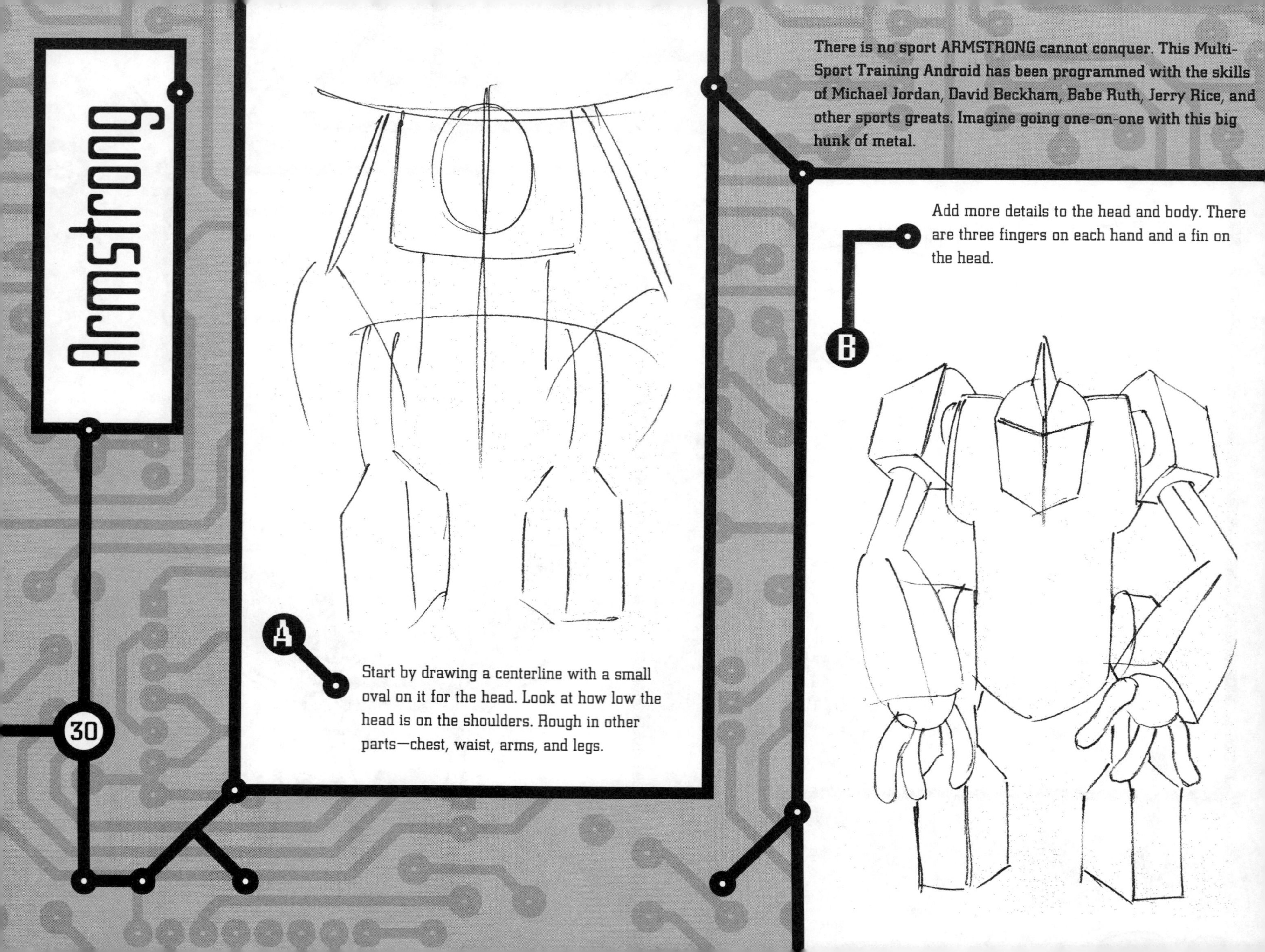

Armstrong

There is no sport ARMSTRONG cannot conquer. This Multi-Sport Training Android has been programmed with the skills of Michael Jordan, David Beckham, Babe Ruth, Jerry Rice, and other sports greats. Imagine going one-on-one with this big hunk of metal.

A

Start by drawing a centerline with a small oval on it for the head. Look at how low the head is on the shoulders. Rough in other parts—chest, waist, arms, and legs.

B

Add more details to the head and body. There are three fingers on each hand and a fin on the head.

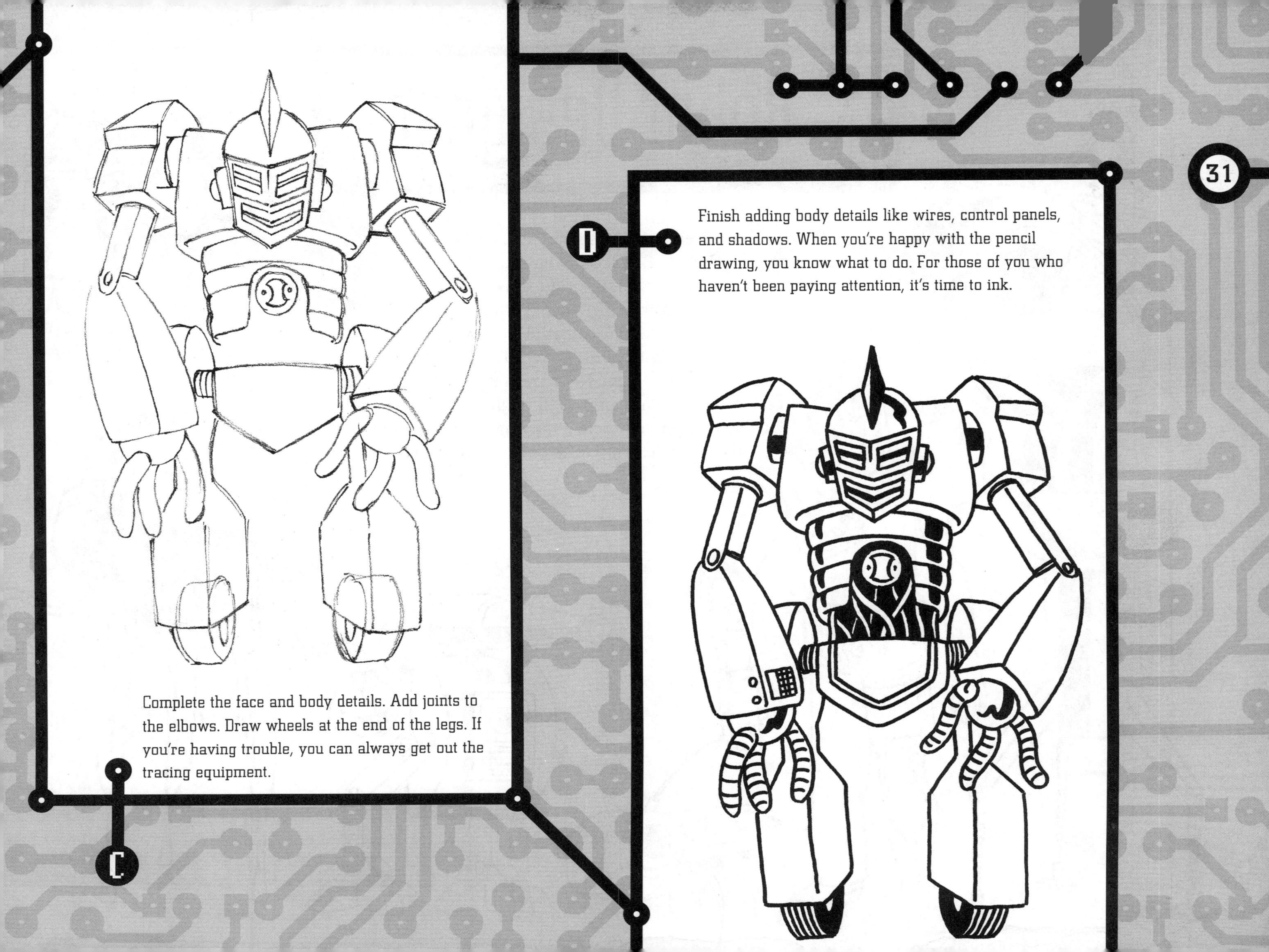

C

Complete the face and body details. Add joints to the elbows. Draw wheels at the end of the legs. If you're having trouble, you can always get out the tracing equipment.

D

Finish adding body details like wires, control panels, and shadows. When you're happy with the pencil drawing, you know what to do. For those of you who haven't been paying attention, it's time to ink.

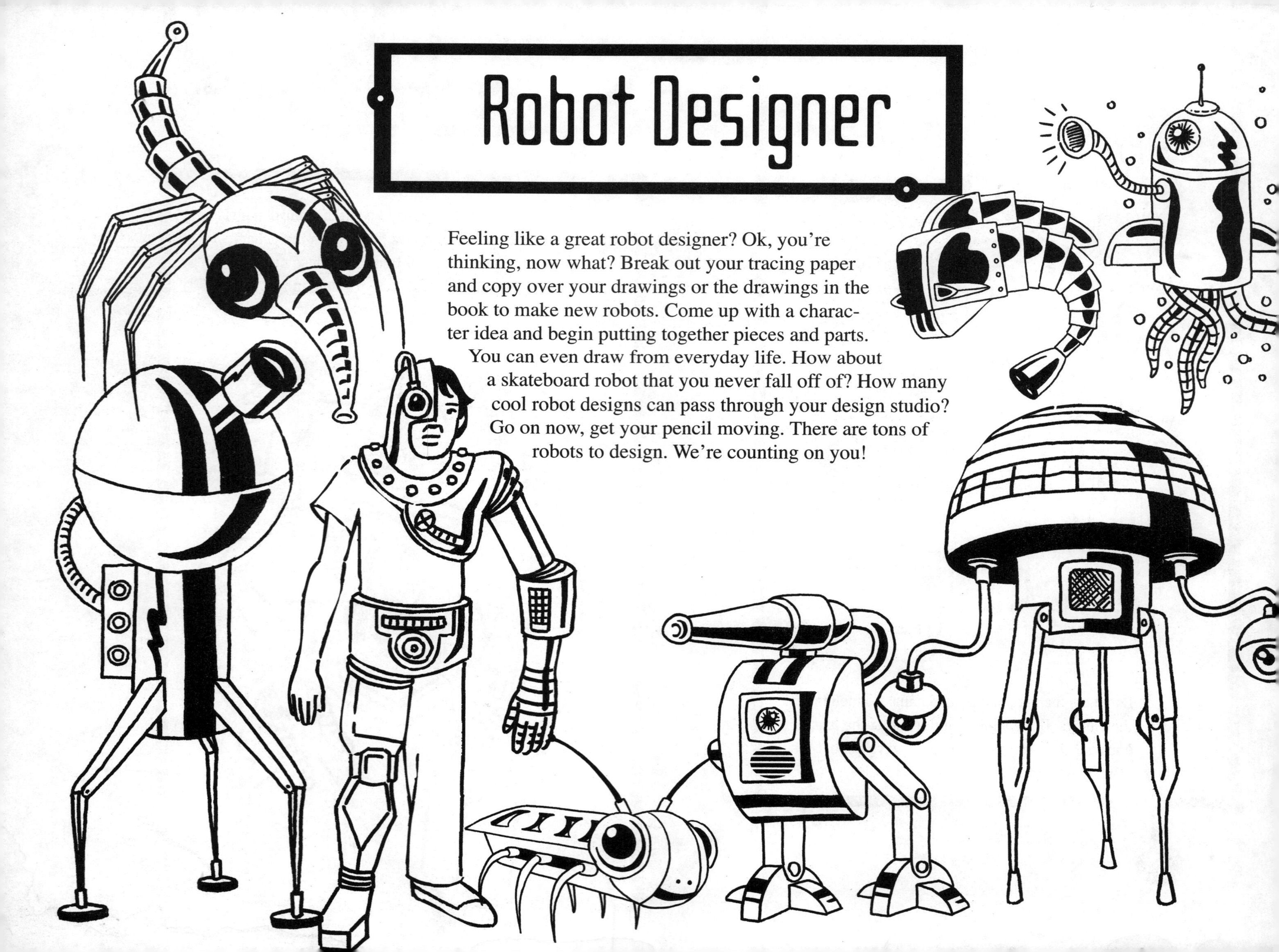

Robot Designer

Feeling like a great robot designer? Ok, you're thinking, now what? Break out your tracing paper and copy over your drawings or the drawings in the book to make new robots. Come up with a character idea and begin putting together pieces and parts. You can even draw from everyday life. How about a skateboard robot that you never fall off of? How many cool robot designs can pass through your design studio? Go on now, get your pencil moving. There are tons of robots to design. We're counting on you!